ASIA REDUX

The **Nalanda-Sriwijaya Centre (NSC)** at the Institute of Southeast Asian Studies, Singapore, pursues research on historical interactions among Asian societies and civilizations. It serves as a forum for comprehensive study of the ways in which Asian polities and societies have interacted over time through religious, cultural, and economic exchanges and diasporic networks. The Research Series provides scholars with an avenue to present the outcome of their research and allows an opportunity to develop new or innovative approaches in the sphere of intra-Asian interactions.

The **Institute of Southeast Asian Studies (ISEAS)** was established as an autonomous organization in 1968. It is a regional centre dedicated to the study of socio-political, security and economic trends and developments in Southeast Asia and its wider geostrategic and economic environment. The Institute's research programmes are the Regional Economic Studies (RES, including ASEAN and APEC), Regional Strategic and Political Studies (RSPS), and Regional Social and Cultural Studies (RSCS).

ISEAS Publishing, an established academic press, has issued more than 2,000 books and journals. It is the largest scholarly publisher of research about Southeast Asia from within the region. ISEAS Publishing works with many other academic and trade publishers and distributors to disseminate important research and analyses from and about Southeast Asia to the rest of the world.

NALANDA SRIWIJAYA CENTRE
Institute of Southeast Asian Studies
SINGAPORE
RESEARCH SERIES

Asia Redux

Conceptualising a Region for Our Times

Edited by

Prasenjit Duara

With contributions by

Sugata Bose, Jennifer Munger, Wang Hui, Tansen Sen, Amitav Acharya, Barbara Watson Andaya, Rudolf Mrázek

ISEAS
INSTITUTE OF SOUTHEAST ASIAN STUDIES
Singapore

MANOHAR

First published in Singapore in 2013
by ISEAS Publishing
Institute of Southeast Asian Studies
30 Heng Mui Keng Terrace, Pasir Panjang
Singapore 119614
E-mail: publish@iseas.edu.sg
Website: http://bookshop.iseas.edu.sg
for distribution in all countries except South Asia

Published by Manohar Publishers & Distributors
4753/23, Ansari Road, Daryaganj, New Delhi 110002
for distribution in South Asia

Originally published in the *Journal of Asian Studies*, Volume 69, Number 4 (November 2010)

ISEAS Library Cataloguing in Publication Data

Asia redux : conceptualising a region for our times / edited by Prasenjit Duara.
Regionalism—Asia.
Asia—Foreign relations.
Asia—History.
Duara, Prasenjit.

JZ5333 A831 2013

ISBN 978-981-4414-49-4 (hard cover)
ISBN 978-981-4414-51-7 (e-book, PDF)

Cover photo: Map of Asia, 1808. Source: *The General Gazetteer; or Compendious Geographical Dictionary* by R. Brookes. Eighth Edition. Dublin, 1808.

Typeset by Manohar Publishers.
Printed at Salasar Imaging Systems, Delhi 110035

Contents

Preface

SUGATA BOSE

A world-historical transformation is under way in the early twenty-first century as Asia recovers the global position it had lost in the late eighteenth century. Yet the idea of Asia and a spirit of Asian universalism were alive and articulated in a variety of registers during the period of European imperial domination. One of the most creative exponents of an Asia-sense was Rabindranath Tagore (1861-1941) who won the Nobel Prize for Literature in 1913. "Each country of Asia will solve its own historical problems according to its strength, nature and need," Tagore said during a visit to Iran in 1932, "but the lamp that they will each carry on their path to progress will converge to illuminate the common ray of knowledge... it is only when the light of the spirit glows that the bond of humanity becomes true."[1]

In my book *A Hundred Horizons* I had claimed that Tagore was an eloquent proponent of a universalist aspiration, albeit a universalism with a difference.[2] This specific claim was part of a larger contention that modern history could be interpreted – not wholly or in full measure, but very substantially – as an interplay of multiple and competing universalisms. The colonized did not simply erect defensive walls around their notions of cultural difference. They were keen to be players in broad arenas of cosmopolitan thought zones and wished to contribute to the shaping of a global future.

The spirit of different universalism that appealed to anti-colonial nationalists in Asia may have been water-borne as it traveled through sea voyages across the Indian Ocean, but was never quite defined by an expanse of water except in a metaphorical sense. It is best in this context not to exaggerate the contradiction between oceans and continents that

---

[1] Sugata Bose, *A Hundred Horizons: the Indian Ocean in the Age of Global Empire* (Cambridge, MA: Harvard University Press, 2006), p. 265.

[2] Bose, *A Hundred Horizons*, pp. 267-70.

has crept into some of the scholarly literature. The myth of continents has been subjected to a powerful indictment with some justice as a meta-geographical concept hopelessly tainted by the hubris of European imperialism.[3] The idea of Asia, however, or of Africa, I might venture to add, was not a singular one and had almost as many variations as it had individual authors. More important, Asian universalism as articulated by Asians was certainly at variance with the concrete expression of Asia invented by nineteenth-century European geographers and cartographers. There were strands within Asian thought-worlds that merely inverted and did not undermine the Europe-Asia dichotomy, being content to invest the latter with a higher order of value and virtue. That forms a less interesting dimension of the modern tug-of-war between Europe and Asia. Far more fascinating was the imagination of Asia as an abstract entity transcending the imperial and national frontiers being etched by colonial powers on to the physical and mental maps of the colonized, and thereby serving as a prism to refract the light of universal humanity.

The exchange of views among scholars of Asia triggered by Prasenjit Duara's stimulating think piece "Asia Redux" contains a set of valuable insights into forms of spatial imagination in modern history. Duara's opening salvo has the merit of creatively integrating an analysis of economic networks with an exploration of a cultural ecumene. Dealing with the concepts of region and regionalization with great theoretical finesse, he is able to evoke the history of pre-modern and modern intra-Asian connections in the domain of material life and cultural conceptions of Asia forged in response to European imperialism within a common explanatory framework. Duara's essay is of great topical salience in our contemporary global moment.

Each of the responses opens up fresh avenues for reflection and research. Wang Hui perceptively notes how a re-conceptualization of Asia can never be divorced from a reconsideration of the idea of Europe and world history. Tansen Sen reminds us that land routes complemented sea-lanes in forging intra-Asian links in pre-modern times. This is equally true of the modern

---

[3] Martin Lewis and Karen Wigen, *The Myth of Continents: A Critique of Metageography* (Berkeley: University of California Press, 1997).

era. It is important to recognize that there were inter-regional arenas of human interactions transcending imperial and national boundaries over land and across seas. Sen also cautions us against over-romanticizing the nature of pre-modern connections by pointing to episodes of war and violent conflict. Yet these instances, as Duara notes, appear to be exceptions rather than the rule. The flows of culture and commerce proved resilient to the occasional violent ruptures. Moreover, the strategic essentializing in the modern era by poet-philosophers like Tagore, who emphasized intellectual and cultural interactions and downplayed military aggression in the past, is interesting of itself in expressing an ethical preference for the present and the future.

Amitava Acharya powerfully broaches the concept of regionalism as distinct from region and regionalization in thinking about Asia. The title of his response – "Asia is Not One" – appears to be a bit of a misnomer. What he really shows is that there were multiple articulations and alternative visions of the famous claim, first made by Okakura in 1901, that "Asia is one". The distinctions and imbrications between the concepts of nationalist Asia, universalist Asia and regionalist Asia offer an innovative way forward in writing a new history of political and economic ideas that circulated across Asia and beyond.

If the forces of contemporary globalization have a dark under-belly, so do the flows that constitute an Asian or Indian Ocean inter-regional arena. Rudolf Mrázek underscores the need to train the spotlight on labor migration as well as the dialectic between mobility and immobility. Indentured migrant labor in mines and plantations was a key feature of Asia in the age of European colonial empires even as settled and sedentary peasant labor toiled on smallholdings. A post-imperialist and potentially post-nationalist Asia must do better.

Duara in his final word pleads guilty to the charge of indulging in advocacy. Taking a normative position after sifting through all the historical evidence does not necessarily undermine the standards of scholarly objectivity. In re-envisioning the idea of Asia in the Asian century it makes sense to take a stand on the side of a generous universalism against the hubris of an arrogant imperialism and narrow nationalism. The best Asian thinkers of the last two centuries did just that.

Introduction

JENNIFER MUNGER

The papers in this publication began as a discussion between *Journal of Asian Studies* editor Jeffrey Wasserstrom and author Prasenjit Duara, who wrote a think piece for the journal entitled "Asia Redux: Conceptualizing a Region for Our Times." Early on, the two agreed that the paper should be published with commentaries, along the lines of the Rule of Law forum spanning India and China in volume 68: 1 (February 2009). The topics of the paper, which include the ways in which the area we call Asia has been interconnected in the nineteenth and twentieth centuries and how it has been conceptualized as a coherent region by Asian intellectuals in the last century, fit in well with the unique aim of the *Journal of Asian Studies* in cultivating a common ground for discussions that encompass broad issues and regions in Asia. This paper in particular gives scholars the opportunity to problematise conceptions of what constitutes Asia.

As the discussion about how to proceed and who to include in a forum progressed, we at the editorial office found it appealing to expand the idea by hosting a roundtable discussion at the Association for Asian Studies meeting in Philadelphia in the spring of 2010, held as a meeting in conjunction rather than as a formal panel. As Moderator, I asked participants to consider two broad questions: what constitutes Asia, and what attributes or processes serve to allow Asia as a whole, or areas within Asia, to be considered under a single rubric. The working title for the event was "What Makes an Area an Asia," though over the course of time, and in the conference programme it became "What Makes an Area in Asia." Either question serves as a useful basis for discussion.

Our goals were to find commentators from a range of disciplines and backgrounds so as to explore and critique the ideas presented in Duara's essay. We sought scholars who had a broad vision and whose work addressed political and/or identity formation in some way. To that end, we invited Kären Wigen, Professor of History and Director of the Center for East Asian Studies at Stanford University, whose work focuses on Japanese studies and geography as reflected in the book she co-wrote with Martin Lewis entitled *The Myth of Continents: A Critique of Metageography* (1997); Wang Hui, Professor of Chinese Language and Literature at Tsinghua University and former editor of *Dushu* and the *New Leftist;* Tansen Sen, historian at Baruch College, CUNY, whose expertise spans China, Japan, India and Buddhism, and author of *Buddhism, Diplomacy, and Trade: The Realignment of Sino-Indian Relations, 600-1400* (2003); Rudolf Mrázek, scholar of modern Indonesia and history at the University of Michigan and author of *Engineers of Happy Land: Technology and Nationalism in a Colony* (2002); and Barbara Watson Andaya, Professor of Asian Studies and Director of the Center for Southeast Asian Studies at the University of Hawaii at Mānoa, President of the Association of Asian Studies in 2005–06 and author of *The Flaming Womb: Repositioning Women in Southeast Asian History* (2006). We had also invited Howard French, Associate Professor of Journalism at Columbia University, former *New York Times* Shanghai bureau chief, and the author of *A Continent for the Taking: The Tragedy and Hope of Africa* (2003) to participate, but in the end, he was unable to attend.

To prepare for the roundtable, we circulated Duara's full paper to all of the commentators. We advertised the event on the Association for Asian Studies website (among other venues) and posted a summary statement and quotes from the paper on the site to generate interest and provide talking points, since the paper would not be read at the roundtable discussion. At the forum, Prasenjit Duara made a brief introduction of his work, followed by commentaries by each of the respondents. Attendance at the forum was large, with more than 30 people. As was expected and hoped for, a variety of issues came up in the course of the presenters' discussions. Kären Wigen, who was unable to join in the published comments but participated in the roundtable, used maps to help illustrate how the representation of geography is used to define place. Wigen pointed out that externally imposed maps delineating regions in Asia have become, over time, indigenised to the point where it is moot to consider such mapping as foreign; that framing questions in terms of the regions of Asia as externally produced misses important avenues of investigation and understanding. The debate after the presentations (which will be introduced below) was very lively and satisfying. Notably, Donald Emmerson, Director of the Southeast Asia Forum and Senior Fellow at the Freeman Spogli Institute for International Studies at Stanford University, commented on the importance of imagination and subjectivity in considering the topic of Asia, and Amitav Acharya (whose written comments are addressed below) focused on the importance of process over essential qualities as a key factor in considering Asia, emphasising moments of time as key in the determination of space. The session ended with an excellent summation by Robert Cribb, Professor in the School of Culture, History & Language at the Australian National University, which is that the factor which makes Asia an area is dependent on one's research agenda. What makes Asia is drawn different ways depending on the questions we ask.

What follows this introduction are the printed versions of the comments of invited participants in the roundtable, with the addition of Amitav Acharya, Professor in the School of International Service at the American University, Washington D.C. and author of *Whose Ideas Matter: Agency and Power in Asian Regionalism* (2009). These comments were originally published in the *Journal of Asian Studies* 69: 4 (November 2010). Wang Hui asserts that Asia cannot be considered as an idea without problematizing the notion of Europe and reconsidering the history of world interactions and power dynamics. Tansen Sen concurs that a broader global picture is needed to understand Asia, a picture that could be better fleshed out by examining earlier maritime records and by recognizing that war and conflict play important roles in making an area an Asia. In his written remarks, Amitav Acharya emphasizes five different but overlapping visions of consciously directed actions to form Asian commonalities and identity. Barbara Watson Andaya takes an ethnographic perspective in examining cultural flows, in particular religion, which can be both manipulated by nation states to foster local identity while also being universalist in ideology, a combination which makes for a fluid tool in viewing Asia dynamically in time and space. Rudolf Mrázek provocatively warns that by viewing Asia as steady rhythmic flows, we do injustice to the messy reality of history, leaving too many questions unanswered.

The forum and subsequent publication generated considerable interest. Tansen Sen proposed presenting the works as a small book for distribution in Asia with the idea of promoting the study of intra-Asian interactions. Warm thanks to him and to Cambridge University Press, publisher of the *Journal of Asian Studies,* for making this possible.

Asia Redux: Conceptualizing a Region for Our Times

PRASENJIT DUARA

How has Asia appeared as a region and been conceived as such in the last hundred years? While there is a longstanding and still burgeoning historiography of Asian connections through the study of the precolonial and early modern maritime trade, the nineteenth and twentieth centuries are generally not seen as a time of growing Asian connections. The recent rise of interest in Asian connections in the current time is thus unable to grasp the continuities and discontinuities that form the present. Even more, it is unable to evaluate the risks and possibilities of the present moment.

Before launching upon the subject, we need to question how, where, and why a region appears. I will approach this question from the perspective of historical sociology. Scholars have made a useful distinction between a region and regionalization, distinguishing between the relatively unplanned or evolutionary emergence of an area of interaction and interdependence as a "region," and the more active, often ideologically driven political process of creating a region, or "regionalization."

While understanding the history of the concept of the Asian region requires us to utilize both of these conceptions and their complex interactions, I believe that there is a more fundamental issue underlying why regions and regionalisms succeed or fail, and also why they take the shape they do, as few will argue that the Asian region reflects a cartographic representation of Asia. After all, Asia was merely the name of the area east of the Greek *ecumene* in ancient times. I hypothesize that regions and regionalizations tend to follow the dominant or hegemonic modes of *spatial production* during a period. For the twentieth century, the paradigm of large-scale production of social space was the territorial nation state under conditions of global capitalist production and exchange. Note that this way of formulating the problem may also incorporate the socialist nation state, which sought to industrialize under conditions of global capital accumulation.

In Henri Lefebvre's classic study, he shows how powerful systems such as capitalism produce the kinds of space they require.[1] These spaces are constituted by relationships that can be abstracted, standardized, exchanged, and secured by property rights. In capitalist space, physical factors of production such as land and water become commodities. National spaces are often continuous with this kind of space, which the nation state authorises not only by guaranteeing property rights, but also by seeking to homogenize the population as citizens with overarching loyalty not to their substantive communities or life worlds, but to the national community through the nation state. This homogenizing tendency of the nation state may, of course, be reproduced within nested formations in which horizontal identity is expressed in associations, provinces, language groups, and so on, theoretically under the sovereign nation state. *In the national model of space, there is an effort to make culture and political authority congruent.* Of course, this also produces tensions between national and capitalist space. Most significantly, the territorial sovereignty of the nation state can limit the deterritorializing imperative of capitalism.

IMPERIAL REGIONALISM

During the nineteenth and twentieth centuries, the relationship between global capitalism, regional formations, and the nation state was mediated by imperialism. Much of nineteenth-century Asia was dominated by the "free trade" imperialism of the British Empire, at a time when several historical networks of the Asian maritime trade were able to adapt and expand their operations. By the late nineteenth century and during the first half of the twentieth century, imperialism came to be driven by nationalism to compete effectively in a capitalist system, whether this was to secure resources, markets, or the military needs of the capitalist nation. This yielded a complex relationship between imperialist nations

[1] Henri Lefebvre, *The Production of Space*, trans. Donald Nicholson-Smith (Oxford: Blackwell, 1992).

and their colonial or dependent territories, which they sought to develop as imperial regions.[2]

Turning first to the nineteenth century, colonial empires, most notably the British Empire, created significant regional interdependencies in Asia. This had the effect of intensifying some of the old relationships and generating new linkages between the cities (and hinterlands) of Aden, Bombay, Calcutta, Singapore, Hong Kong, and Shanghai as entrepôts and financial centres for Asian trade. For a long time, the study of Asian trade in the colonial period was conducted apart from the rich and high-quality scholarship of the precolonial maritime Asian or Indian Ocean trade, thus yielding a skewed picture of the former. It was perhaps taken for granted that the financial, technological, and political-military superiority of the colonial powers in the nineteenth century had completely subordinated, if not eliminated, these networks. This seems to have been the assumption behind the dual economy model of J.H. Boeke and others. More recent work on the Indian Ocean—along the Gulf of Aden and Arabian Sea as well as the South China Sea—has shown how faulty this picture was.

Since at least the thirteenth century, the maritime region from the Red Sea to the South China Sea represented an interlinked system of trade routes. From the 1400s, the routes were held together, most importantly, by the cosmopolitan port city of Malacca, to which the monsoon winds brought Indian, Persian, and Arab traders. There, they waited for the reversal of the monsoon winds to carry in the trade from the Chinese empire and eastern regions before returning. The networks of Chinese, Indian, Jewish, and Arab merchants, among others,with their sophisticated credit transfer mechanisms and trading techniques enabled the

---

[2] See Eric J. Hobsbawm, *Nations and Nationalism since 1780: Programme, Myth, Reality* (Cambridge: Cambridge University Press, 1990), 102; and Hannah Arendt, *The Origins of Totalitarianism* (New York: Harcourt Brace Jovanovich, 1973), 152–53. Arguably, even after World War II, during the Cold War, the political mechanism that was developed to compete for global resources was national imperialism, or the means whereby a national superpower exercised its hegemony over subordinated nation states.

wholesale and forward carrying trade across the Indian Ocean littoral from Zanzibar to China.[3]

According to Rajat K. Ray, while Asian networks from the nineteenth century were doubtless subordinated to colonial trade and power, the older networks of Chinese, Indian, and (Baghdadi) Jewish communities, which possessed long-distance credit networks and negotiable financial instruments operable in several countries, adapted and expanded their operations within certain spheres. Their business practices enabled them to occupy a realm between the European world of banks and corporations and the small Asian peddler and retail markets. Indeed, without the financial and marketing services provided by these mobile merchant communities of Asia, European capital would not have been able to penetrate the hinterlands. During the course of the twentieth century, not only did these networks expand into the lower latitudes of Africa and Southeast Asia, but also they emerged as the modern Asian business and industrial classes, which were able to integrate the three-tiered colonial economies into national and postnational economies.[4]

On the East Asian side, the multiple connections and shifts between the precolonial maritime networks and modern Asian networks has been studied masterfully by Hamashita Takeshi. By the Qing period, the Chinese imperial tribute system had become the framework for commercial transactions based on the price structure in China. The entire tribute trade zone became loosely integrated by the use of silver as a medium of trade settlement. It became the axis around which wider trading networks in

---

[3] Rajat K. Ray, "Asian Capital in the Age of European Expansion: The Rise of the Bazaàr, 1800–1914," *Modern Asian Studies* 29, no. 3 (1995): 449–554, 464, 472; Janet Lippman Abu-Lughod, "The World System in the Thirteenth Century: Dead-End or Precursor?" in *Essays on Global and Comparative History,* edited by Michael Adas (Washington, D.C.: American Historical Association, 1993), 9–11. For the precolonial Asian networks, see also the magisterial study of K.N. Chaudhuri, *Asia before Europe: Economy and Civilization of the Indian Ocean from the Rise of Islam to 1750* (Cambridge: Cambridge University Press, 1990).

[4] Ray, "Asian Capital in the Age of European Expansion," 553; see also Sugata Bose, *A Hundred Horizons: The Indian Ocean in the Age of Global Empire* (Cambridge, Mass.: Harvard University Press, 2006).

the region were organised. Thus, for instance, the private trade between Siam and South China was fueled by profits from tribute mission, and when trade in this region declined, traders in South China were able to switch to trading alongside other tribute missions, say, from Ryukyu to Nagasaki. Tribute trade also linked the European trade with the East Asian one. While it may have appeared to be an exclusively political relationship, in reality, the tribute system also expressed trading opportunities under a loose regulatory system of several different states within an imperial Chinese tribute zone.[5] Not only has Hamashita shown how European-dominated patterns rode on older networks of Asian trade, he also has recently revealed what he calls the "crossed networks" (*kōsanettowaku*) of Chinese and Indian overseas financial groups in East, South, and Southeast Asia.[6] The Japanese conquests and the partial overtaking of control of this trade opened new opportunities for regional integration, but it turned out to be more destructive than enabling during the short period it existed.

Moving on to imperial regional formation in the interwar years of the twentieth century, national imperialisms sought to develop a regional or (geographically dispersed) bloc formation promoting economic autarky as a means for the imperial power to gain global supremacy or advantage. Here they sought to establish common standards, measures, currency, and laws to facilitate integration—if uneven development—across the bloc. After World War I, the indebtedness of Great Britain to the United States and its weakening competitiveness vis-à-vis other imperialist powers caused the British to impose the doctrine of imperial preference and the sterling zone in its colonies and dependencies. This was also, however, a

---

[5] Hamashita Takeshi,"The Tribute Trade System and Modern Asia," in *Japanese Industrialization and the Asian Economy*, edited by A.J.H. Latham and Heita Kawasatsu (London: Routledge, 1994).

[6] Hamashita Takeshi, "Kōsa suru Indokei nettowaku to Kajinkei nettowaku: Honkoku sōkin shisutemu no hikaku kentō" [Intersecting Networks of Indians and Chinese: A Comparative Investigation of the Remittance System], in *Gendai Minami Ajia 6: Sekai Sisutemu To Nettowâku* [Contemporary South Asia 6: World System and Network], ed. Akita Shigeru and Mizushima (Tokyo: Tokyo University Press, 2003), 239–74.

time when the anti-imperialist movement in the colonies began to make increasing demands for economic and political parity. Thus, imperialists sought to create economic blocs in which colonies or subordinate territories were promised self-governing status and other concessions, and sometimes were even constituted as nominally sovereign nation states, although they remained militarily in thrall to the metropole. The imperialism of nation states reflected a strategic reorientation of the periphery to be part of an organic formation designed to attain global supremacy for the imperial power. As Albert Lebrun declared after World War I, the goal was now to "unite France to all those distant Frances in order to permit them to combine their efforts to draw from one another reciprocal advantages."[7]

But it was less the older imperialist powers than the new ones such as Japan, the United States, and the Soviet Union that proved able to switch to this mode of regional imperialism of nation states. With the increased need for resource and social mobilization within colonies or dependencies, it was more efficient for the imperialists to foster *modern* and *indirectly* controlled institutions in them. The goal was to control these areas by dominating their institutions of mobilization, such as banks, transportation infrastructure, and political institutions, which were created to resemble those of the metropole (such as legislative councils, institutions of political tutelage, and political parties such as the communist parties or the Concordia in Manchukuo). In short, unlike colonialism or British free trade imperialism, the interwar imperialists attended to the modernization of institutions and identities. They often espoused cultural or ideological similarities—including sometimes anticolonial ideologies—even while racism and nationalism accompanied the reality of military-political domination.

To compete with Britain and France, Germany had sought to develop a regional bloc in Central and Eastern Europe since the end of the nineteenth century.[8] This trend accelerated during the interwar years, and German commercial influence before the war peaked in 1938, when Austria was

[7] As quoted in D. Bruce Marshall, *The French Colonial Myth and Constitution-Making in the Fourth Republic* (New Haven, Conn.: Yale University Press, 1973), 44.

[8] Barry Eichengreen and Jeffrey A. Frankel, "Economic Regionalism: Evidence

incorporated into the Reich and Adolf Hitler annexed the Sudeten region of Czechoslovakia. Hannah Arendt regarded the German (and Russian pan-Slav) movement as an expression of "continental imperialism", whereby latecomer nationalists sought to develop their empires through the nationalistic pan-German movement.[9] The German economic New Order in Europe, built on states that were essentially German puppets or had German military governors, was designed to supply the German war effort. However, there were also plans to build an economic region around a prosperous Germany linked to new industrial complexes in central Europe and captured areas of the western Soviet Union. This unitary European market, however, remained a nationalistic German vision—and we should be wary of seeing it as a predecessor of the European Union. The German plan represented in several ways no more than an aborted version of the new imperialism.[10]

Beginning with the formation of the puppet state of Manchukuo (1932–45), the Japanese economic bloc idea grew by the mid-1930s into the East Asian League (*Tōarenmei*) and the East Asian Community (*Tōakyōdōtai*), and still later into the idea of the Greater East Asian Co-Prosperity Sphere (*Dai-Tōakyōeiken*). Manchukuo signalled fundamental changes in the nature of the Japanese empire. The truly intensive phase of industrialization and development in Korea and Taiwan came after 1931 and emerged as part of the plan for strategic autarky centred on Manchukuo. The rapid growth in industrialization, education, and other aspects of development in Korea and Taiwan began mostly in the early 1930s, and accelerated with the invasion of China in 1937. The Japanese

---

from Two Twentieth-Century Episodes," *North American Journal of Economics and Finance* 6, no. 2 (1995): 97.

[9] Arendt, *The Origins of Totalitarianism*, 222–23. This racist ideology seemingly authorized the Germans to annex or dominate territories belonging to other states. At the same time, Nazi racism excluded such large numbers of people that even the rhetoric of anti-imperialism or solidarity of cultures was made impossible.

[10] See Richard Overy, "World Trade and World Economy," in *The Oxford Companion to World War II*, edited by Ian C.B. Dear and M.R.D. Foot (Oxford: Oxford University Press, 2001).

wartime empire resembled the German New Order in that the entire occupied zone became subordinated to Japanese war needs, and Japan's defeat represented a failure of the new imperialism.[11]

This form of imperial regionalism, then, was characterized by an unsustainable tension: a commitment to creating a common space akin to the nation that would extend the benefits and pains of creating a globally competitive region, but would extend them *unevenly* over the whole. By the same token, the imperial-national region was often ripped apart by enduring nationalist prejudices fostered in earlier times and simultaneous processes of nation building, especially within the imperial metropole. In other words, while it sought to create a region of interdependence and cooperation, the national interests of the imperial power made this an unsustainable region.

What was the spatial composition of this imperialist region? While most of the subordinate nations or colonies within the region were by no means fully integrated with capitalist urban centres, the infrastructure of capitalist market relations—including standardization of weights and measures, currency unification, and the physical and educational infrastructure—were being laid across many of these societies, both within each colony or country and across them. The integration was a dual and interactive process undertaken by the colonial states and metropolitan capitalists, as well as by Asian merchants, who, as shown earlier, dominated the indigenous financial markets through bills of exchange, promissory notes, and other negotiable instruments (such as the Chinese *gu* or South Asian *hundis*). As Hamashita has shown, Singapore and Hong Kong were colonial cities in which the Chinese and Indian money transfer and remittance networks intersected, and their resources became part of a vast regional financial market interfluent with the Western-dominated banking sector.[12] But if the material lives and economic practices of Asians were

---

[11] For Manchukuo and the Japanese empire, see Prasenjit Duara, *Sovereignty and Authenticity: Manchukuo and the East Asian Modern* (Boulder, CO: Rowman and Littlefied, 2003).

[12] Hamashita, "Kōsa suru Indokei nettowaku to Kajinkei nettowaku," 261–67.

becoming interlinked on an everyday basis, how was this reflected in the representation of the region?

THE ANTI-IMPERIALIST REGIONALIZATION PROJECT IN ASIA

While the British and Japanese empires were trying to create autarkic, interdependent regions to sustain their imperial power in Asia, anti-imperialist thought linked to rising Asian nationalism was seeking to build an alternative conception of the region. These intellectual proponents of an "Other Asia" evoked earlier linkages between their societies, but it should be noted that their conceptualization of Asia was itself premised and enabled by contemporary imperialist technologies and modes of regional integration.

The idea of Asia among these Asians was expressed largely through a cultural movement that is instructive for us to explore. I will review here the efforts of three intellectuals—Okakura Tenshin, Rabindranath Tagore, and Zhang Taiyan—as in this early period, Asianism was principally an intellectual and cultural effort until it was overtaken by the Japanese military for imperialist purposes. Okakura Tenshin or Kakuzo is perhaps most famous for his opening line "Asia is one" in his book *The Ideals of the East with Special Reference to the Arts of Japan,* written in 1901 (published 1903).[13] Okakura, who was deeply knowledgeable about Chinese art and culture and closely connected with South Asian Asianists such as Tagore and Ananda Coomaraswamy, as well as with American art entrepreneurs such as Ernest Fenellosa, probably did more than anyone to establish Asian art as a legitimate and viable domain of high art, fit for museums and the art market.

It was through his conception of the great civilizational arts of China and India, and not least the aesthetic values of Buddhism, that Okakura saw the unity of the Asian ideals that reigned before what he regarded as the marauding of the Mongols and their successors. But even as Okakura was articulating the ideal of Asia, in the same moment, he was also carving

[13] Okakura Tenshin, *The Ideals of the East with Special Reference to the Arts of Japan* (Tokyo: ICG Muse, 2002).

out a place for Japan in the civilized world of the West as the inheritor and leader of this present fallen Asia. Okakura saw Japan as a survivor and a leader. "Thus Japan is a museum of Asiatic civilization and yet more than a museum, because the singular genius of the race leads it to dwell on all phases of the ideals of the past, in that spirit of living Advaitism which welcomes the new without losing the old."[14] The temples of Nara reveal that the great art of the Tang and the much older influence of Shang workmanship can also be found in Japan.

Rabindranath Tagore and Okakura had a close friendship, and Okakura spent considerable time in India, acquiring a deep respect for its arts and culture even while introducing the utterly fascinated circle in the Tagore house, Jorasankho, to Chinese and Japanese culture. Both men sought to live their lives according to their ideals, even donning the clothing of their historical cultures while most Western-educated gentlemen were opting for the prestige of the West. Thus, Okakura dressed in a *dhoti* when he visited the Ajanta caves, and Tagore often wore his Daoist hat, given to him during his first China visit. Yet, of course, let it not be forgotten that they possessed the self-confidence to advocate Asian culture because they were so knowledgeable and polished in the arts of the West. Moreover, theirs was sometimes a troubled relationship, in part because Okakura could not quite overcome the social Darwinist presuppositions and imagery of Indian backwardness, and partly because he was an object of exotic curiosity, if not ridicule, among many Indians who had never seen East Asians, particularly in their historical dress.

Some have seen a form of Japanese Orientalism in Okakura's paternalistic attitude toward the older Asian societies. I believe this is an ahistorical impulse. Japanese pan-Asianism at the turn of the century had several different strains, including imperialistic ones, but also egalitarian and compassionate feelings toward fellow Asians who had been exploited and devastated by more aggressive cultures. At the same time, pan-Asianism cultivated a deep claim of Japanese leadership in Asia and a self-imputed responsibility to raise Asians from their fallen state. Okakura saw Japan as the hall or museum—the enabler—that would display all of the

---

[14] Okakura Tenshin, *The Ideals of the East*, 7–8.

different civilizations of Asia. This enabling role, of course, could easily be transformed into a superiority and instrumentalization of what it enabled. It was this tendency—or what we might call a "structure of feeling"—that grew into the ideological foundations of Japanese imperialism, endowing it with the mission to lead Asians. Indeed, as is well known, it is the subservience of pan-Asianism to Japanese militarist imperialism that doomed its future in the twentieth century.

Zhang Taiyan or Zhang Binglin is widely considered to be one of the most powerful intellectuals of late Qing and early Republican China. The great writer Lu Xun certainly regarded him as such and saw himself as a lifelong student of Zhang. Many see Zhang as a maverick thinker who was both narrowly racist in his violent anti-Manchu revolutionary views and deeply humanist and learned—being not only the foremost scholar of ancient Chinese learning, but also widely read in Buddhist philosophy, especially the Yogacārā or Consciousness-Only (*weishi* or *vijnapatimatra*) school of Buddhism, of which he was a practitioner.

Zhang became committed to Buddhism during his years in jail (1903–06) as a result of his revolutionary activities. He suffered greatly in jail and watched his younger colleague Zou Rong die under terrible privation. He claimed that he was saved only by his voracious readings of Buddhist philosophy. We do not have the time here to discuss the allegation of the maverick's inconsistency except to indicate that *alaya* (storehouse) thinking permitted different levels of consciousness and commitment depending on the needs of the time. This philosophy disposes one to think very differently from the principle of commitment to ethical consistency.

Zhang espoused the cause of freedom from imperialism in Asia while in Japan after his release from prison. There, he attended the meetings of the Indian freedom fighters commemorating the birth anniversary of the Maratha warrior Shivaji, who had fought against the Moguls. He is said to have authored the manifesto of the Asian Solidarity Society created in Tokyo around 1907. It begins thus:

> Among the various Asian countries, India has Buddhism and Hinduism; China has the theories of Confucius, Mencius, Lao Zi, Zhuang Zi and Yang Zi; then moving to Persia, they also have enlightened religions, such as Zoroastrianism. The various races in this region had self-respect and did

> not invade one another . . . They rarely invaded one another and treated each other respectfully with the Confucian virtue of benevolence. About one hundred years ago, the Europeans moved east and Asia's power diminished day by day. Not only was their political and military power totally lacking, but people also felt inferior. Their scholarship deteriorated and people only strove after material interests.[15]

Zhang's Asianism emerged from his commitment to the values of Buddhism, but also from an anti-imperialist position. He saw the threat to peaceful, agrarian societies from warlike cultures. But while committed to the ultimate values of peace, like Okakura, he acknowledged the necessity of creating a modern nation state along the Western model to combat the imperialist powers. Nationalism was a necessary moment in the conception of pan-Asianism.

Only Tagore opposed this position. Tagore was deeply repulsed by nationalism. Writing about nationalism in Japan, he observed, "I have seen in Japan the voluntary submission of the whole people to the trimming of their minds and clipping of their freedoms by their governments . . . The people accept this all-pervading mental slavery with cheerfulness and pride because of their nervous desire to turn themselves into a machine of power, called the Nation, and emulate other machines in their collective worldliness."[16] Tagore's pan-Asianism was deeply affected by his personal friendships in China, but even here, during his last visit in 1929, he was severely attacked by leftist intellectuals and the Kuomintang because of his views.[17] Most of all, he was bitterly disappointed by the growing nationalism of his own homeland in India, where revolutionary nationalists had overtaken the Swadeshi movement that he had once supported. Their growing narrowness—revealed, for instance, in their goal to burn every piece of foreign cloth—had also begun to affect relations between Hindus and Muslims.

---

[15] Viren Murthy, *The Political Philosophy of Zhang Taiyan: The Resistance of Consciousness* (London and Leiden: Brill, 2011).

[16] Rabindranath Tagore, "Nationalism in the West", *Nationalism*, edited by Ramachandra Guha (New Delhi: Penguin Books), 49.

[17] Stephen N. Hay, *Asian Ideas of East and West: Tagore and His Critics in Japan, China, and India* (Cambridge, Mass.: Harvard University Press, 1970), 323–24.

Tagore was committed to an alternative cosmopolitanism drawn from Asian traditions, which he sought to realize in Vishwa Bharati (India of the World) University at Santiniketan. According to Saranindranath Tagore, Tagore's philosophy of education rose above both abstract and lifeless rationalism as well as violent nationalism and particularism. He was persuaded that reason would emerge only after a primary identification with an inherited tradition. Education would have to nurture the attitude of seeking reason to bridge radical differences by recognizing the consciousness of humanity's latent oneness.[18] One of the great hopes of Santiniketan was realized with the institution of Cheena Bhavan (China Hall) initiated by scholar Tan Yunshan, whose children, notably Tan Chung, remain cultural ambassadors between China and India. Among others, Tagore's own relatives were pioneers in introducing Chinese arts and scholarship to Indians.

Tagore's cosmopolitanism, which he derived from the Advaita or monistic philosophical tradition, has some unexpected parallels with contemporary thinkers from different traditions, such as Jürgen Habermas. Tagore's commitment to the universality of reason as made possible by working through difference resembles Habermas's idea of communicative rationality as emerging from the negotiation of various value claims of different groups and communities. But as with Habermas's theory of communicative rationality, Tagore's educational philosophy could not withstand power—expressed in Tagore's case in the historical force of nationalism and allied ideologies. The logic of communicative acts and education is not the only or dominant logic of society—the logic of power often frames this discussion through reified expressions of community (as in nationalisms or communal religion). For most of the century, while Tagore was celebrated, his cosmopolitan educational project in Santiniketan was ignored and marginalized by the imperatives of a competitive nationalism.

---

[18] Saranindranath Tagore, "Postmodernism and Education: A Tagorean Intervention", paper presented at "Tagore's Philosophy of Education," conference dedicated to the memory of Amita Sen, Kolkata, India, 29–30 March 2006. See also Saranindranath Tagore, "Tagore's Conception of Cosmopolitanism: A Reconstruction," *University of Toronto Quarterly* 77, no. 4 (Fall 2008): 1071-84.

Through this brief survey, we have seen how the three major Asian thinkers were able to conceive of the unity of Asia founded on different principles. The idea of a common historical and religious culture, conceived sometimes as a utopian golden age of peaceful coexistence and dynamic exchange before the arrival of foreign invaders, may have prompted Asianists to think of original Asian value. Note also how in each case, their notion of Asia excluded societies from the Middle East and Central Asia, which each regarded as foreign invaders of their societies. Nonetheless, pan-Asianism, as several scholars have shown, was an important trend in the Middle East as these thinkers reached out especially to Japan as allies against Western imperialism. Indeed, Tagore's four-week visit to Iran in 1932, during which he and his hosts sought to highlight Indo-Iranian civilizational nexus, was perhaps one of his most successful Asian visits.[19] By and large, the three thinkers we have considered were looking for new beginnings in the search for alternative values—alternative to the dominant civilizational narratives of the West. In this sense, they were the founders of a cultural anti-imperialism and articulators of an Asian cosmopolitanism.

However, their thought was ahead of their time, in that it could not be sustained by the political societies in which they lived. Ideas of race, culture, anti-imperialism, and imperialism to be found in pan-Asianism all spelled a lethally close relationship with the dominant trend of nationalism. In the case of Okakura, pan-Asianism became easily absorbed by Japanese imperialism; in the case of Zhang, nationalism took priority because of the circumstances. In the case of Tagore, the nationalism of his time made his ideas and institutions irrelevant for a long period.

The spatial vision of Asia that these thinkers possessed was based not on the actual interactions of people from the different countries—of which there was a great deal—but on an abstract and essentialized notion of culture and civilization formed in the mirror image of the Western concept of civilization. Just as that celebration of the superior achievements of a race and religion—apart from specific classes and areas—worked to further a programme of domination of others, so, too, the idea of Asian civilization was hijacked by Japanese militarism.

[19] Sugata Bose, *A Hundred Horizons,* 260–65.

ASIA AFTER WORLD WAR II

The Cold War division of the world into two camps controlled militarily by nuclear superpowers seeking to dominate the rest of the developing and decolonizing nations may be seen as a kind of supraregionalism. While in fact, the two camps or blocs represented transterritorial spaces including noncontiguous nations, the contiguity of the core Eastern and Western European nations within each camp served as a stepping stone for subsequent regionalism to develop within Europe. We see this tendency as well in Asia, where regional interactions were promoted among the countries of the Central Treaty Organization, the Southeast Asia Treaty Organization, and the Association of Southeast Asian Nations (ASEAN), which were basically security alliances. The Japanese efforts to cultivate Asian markets during and after the Vietnam War also created some economic and cultural grounds for later integration. After the Cold War, ASEAN, which had been designed, unlike the European community, to serve the nation, not only expanded to include the former communist nations of Southeast Asia, but also became more oriented to serve the economic needs of the region.[20] Moreover, places such as Hong Kong, which played an indispensable role as a conduit for exchange between the two camps, were able to reinforce and benefit handsomely from older regional links, especially between Southeast Asia and China.

Another effort to create a regional entity during the early Cold War was the movement of nonaligned nations, principally in Asia, although it also included the African nations. The culmination of this movement was the Bandung Conference, a meeting of the representatives of twenty-nine new nations of Asia and Africa, held in Bandung, Indonesia, in 1955, fifty years after the Russo-Japanese war signalled the beginnings of pan-Asianism. The conference aimed to express solidarity against imperialism and racism and to promote economic and cultural cooperation among these nations. China, India, and Indonesia were key players in the meeting. The conference finally led to the non-aligned movement in 1961, a wider

---

[20] Muthiah Alagappa, *Asian Security Practice: Material and Ideational Influences* (Stanford, Calif.: Stanford University Press, 1998).

third-world force in which participants avowed their distance from the two superpowers—aligning themselves neither with the United States or Soviet Union—during the Cold War. However, conflicts developed among these non-aligned nations—for instance, between India and China in 1962—that eroded the solidarity of the Bandung spirit. At any rate, the non-aligned nations tended to be nationally autarkic in their economic strategies, moving further away from regional linkages.

Thus, all in all, although there were significant foundations for the post-Cold War regionalism to be found in the Cold War itself, the economic energies of the Asian countries in the two camps were directed more toward the nation and the supraregion than the region itself. The congruence between political and cultural realms also came to be directed toward the two loci.

The post-Cold War scene is usually characterized as one of globalization. At the same time, the nation state and nationalism have by no means disappeared; they have developed a new relationship to globalization. In this reconfiguration, regionalism has clearly strengthened, emerging as an intermediate zone between the deterritorializing impulses of capitalism and the territorial limits of nationalism. Evidence of regionalism can be found in Europe, of course, but also in the North American Free Trade Agreement, Mercosur in South America, Asia-Pacific Economic Cooperation, ASEAN (+3 and +6, i.e., the East Asian Summit), and many others. Unlike the Cold War, these are largely economic rather than security-based regionalisms. Moreover, most of these regions are not overwhelmingly dominated by one imperial power or hegemon.

Within East and Southeast Asia—and more recently, India—Asian economic integration has increased significantly, principally since the end of the Asian financial crisis of the late 1990s. The economic integration of East, South, and Southeast Asia, which grew steadily under imperialist-dominated trade, declined precipitously at the end of World War II.[21] Intraregional trade began to pick up in the 1980s, but it was the Asian

[21] Peter A. Petri, "Is East Asia Becoming More Interdependent?" Paper prepared for the session on "European and Asian Integration: Trade and Money Issues," American Economic Association, Boston, 8 January 2005.

financial crisis—the shock of the common crisis—that seems to have awakened states to the reality of regional networks and focused their attention on cooperation. Today, what the Asian Development Bank calls "integrating Asia," including ASEAN, China, Japan, Korea, India, Hong Kong, and Taiwan, conducts more than 50 per cent of its trade among itself, in comparison to trade with the outside world, and compared with only 33 per cent in the 1980s. Six major indicators of interdependence tracked for the sixteen Asian economies have increased markedly in the ten years since the financial crisis.[22]

The most important factor behind the increased trade is the participation of these economies in a regional supply chain production network. Production is divided up into smaller steps, and each part is assigned to the most cost-efficient producer. Thus, for instance, an electronic product may be produced or assembled in China with hardware from Taiwan and software from India. Indeed, much of this type of vertical integration has been enabled by new information and communication technologies and open markets. At the same time, the bulk of these goods have been produced for consumption in Europe and North America. The present crisis in consumption may well lead to deepening markets for these goods within Asia. In recent years, ASEAN has developed free trade agreements with each of the East Asian nations and with India. The China-ASEAN free trade agreement due in 2010 will create the third-largest common market by trade volume. The significantly lower-volume trade between ASEAN and India has also, however, been growing at a compounded annual rate of 27 per cent, and it is likely to accelerate with the signing of the ASEAN-Indian free trade agreement which was signed in August 2009.[23]

---

[22] Asian Development Bank, *Emerging Asian Regionalism: A Partnership for Shared Prosperity* (Manila: Asian Development Bank, 2008), 70, 97–98.

[23] See "Cabinet Nod for ASEAN FTA", *Times of India*, 25 July 2009, http://economictimes.indiatimes.com/News/Economy/Foreign-Trade/Cabinet-nod-for-Asean-FTA/articleshow/4818081.cms (accessed 10 August 2010). On the China-ASEAN free trade agreement, see Collin Spears, "SINO + ASEAN = East Asian Unification? Not Quite Part I," *Brooks Foreign Policy Review*, 20 May 2009,

Financial integration has been relatively weaker within Asia than between individual Asian countries and Western economies. This is particularly noticeable because of the enormous savings generated within Asia that are not productively invested in projects within the region. However, after the 1997–98 financial crisis, the Chiangmai Initiative was undertaken to provide emergency liquidity in case of a foreign exchange crisis in the ASEAN + 3 countries with $80 billion. In 2009, the fund was increased to $120 billion, with Japan and China agreeing to contribute a third each, South Korea putting up 16 per cent, and ASEAN making up the balance of 20 per cent.[24] In the last year, several other countries have entered into bilateral swap agreements. Such agreements have been reached, for instance, between India and Japan, and in response to the precipitous decline of the Korean *won*, Korea recently entered separately into bilateral swap agreements with China and Japan.

Macroeconomic interdependence in the region is also indicated by the movement of macroeconomic variables. For instance, the correlation of gross domestic product (GDP) among many of these states over three-year moving averages is very strong. The GDP correlation coefficient has gone up from 0.07 before the crisis to 0.54 after the crisis. Price movements are similarly correlated, and price shocks in one area are being transmitted to other areas with greater intensity. With the growth of macroeconomic interdependence, a growing need to manage it has appeared. For instance, exchange rates require monitoring and coordination so that central banks do not shoot each other in the foot.[25]

Most of all, of course, the need to coordinate and manage interdependence arises from a common and linked set of problems faced by the region in the realm of climate change, environmental degradation, water scarcity, and public health, among others. The provisioning of these items, which the Asian Development Bank dubs "regional public goods," is evidently urgent. Consider a colossal and dire public goods problem that cannot

---

http://brooksreview.wordpress.com/2009/05/20/sino-asean-east-asian-unification-not-quite-part-i/ (accessed 10 August 2010).

[24] *The Straits Times* (Singapore), Review and Forum, 5 May 2009.

[25] Asian Development Bank, *Emerging Asian Regionalism,* 153–55.

be managed without a concerted regional effort. The Himalayas and the Tibetan Plateau are the source and watershed of ten major rivers that provide freshwater to many different countries in South and Southeast Asia, in addition to China. Climate change and environmental degradation have depleted the water resources available in all these countries, a situation that is particularly severe in north and northwest China, which is suffering the most severe drought in the last half century, with precipitation levels 70 per cent to 90 per cent below normal and water tables depleted from excessive well drilling.[26]

What does this crisis in a remote area of China have to do with South and Southeast Asia? A great deal, in fact. China not only has been building dams on rivers such as the Yangtze, but has also built three more on the Mekong River to produce hydropower for its southwest border regions. About twelve more large dams are expected to be built on the Mekong (or Lancang) alone. Vietnam, Laos, Thailand, and Cambodia have expressed grave concerns about water diversions, shortages, and ecological imbalance in the region. Although China and some authorities assert that the impact of Chinese dam building has not affected downstream waters significantly, the Chinese government has not been very forthcoming with the data on the dams, and it also has not permitted independent scientific studies of the dams. Greater regional efforts must begin with pooling all of the necessary data.[27] Recently, there has been a proposal to divert the waters of several Tibetan rivers, including the Yarlung Tsangpo (Brahmaputra) in India and Bangladesh northward to irrigate the north China plains. The proposal, known as the Great South-North Water Transfer Project, appears to have the backing of President Hu Jintao. Needless to say, the effects of this diversion on South Asia could well lead to unprecedented water wars.[28]

---

[26] Mark Selden, "China's Way Forward? Historical and Contemporary Perspectives on Hegemony and the World Economy in Crisis," *Asia-Pacific Journal,* 24 March 2009.

[27] Geoffrey Gunn and Brian McCartan, "Chinese Dams and the Great Mekong Floods of 2008,"*Japan Focus,* 21 March 2009.

[28] Brahma Chellaney, "China-India Clash over Chinese Claims to Tibetan Water, *Japan Focus,* 3 July 2007.

In this context, it is heartening to learn that economic interdependence within Asia is the major—perhaps the only—factor reducing conflict among these Asian nation states.[29]

THE CIRCULATION OF PEOPLE

I turn now to more direct people-to-people interactions. There is some indication of greater cultural interest of Asians in Asia. We see this in the increase in the number of tourists circulating the region to more than pre-crisis levels. Not only has the market demand for Asian art skyrocketed, but also there are plenty of exhibitions and showings of Asian art in which artists and curators are experimenting with new ideas of Asia as well as art. These shows often deliberately distance themselves from the culturally unified notion of Asia or reified versions of national civilizations prevalent among their predecessors, such as Okakura and Nand Lal Bose. They often seek to showcase the contemporary, urban, multicultural experience of Asia, emphasising heterogeneity and cultural encounters.[30] At a popular level, the circulation of East Asian cinema, manga, anime, television shows, food, design, and allied areas in East and Southeast Asia has been the most conspicuous cultural development in Asia since the 1990s.

Most revealing of the emergent space and complex nature of Asian integration is perhaps the subject of migration and sojourning within the region. Through this optic, we can observe the extent of the move away from the national production of space and explore the possibilities and dangers of a new type of spatial production. As globalization has proceeded over the last two and a half decades, nation states have adopted, albeit to different degrees, strategies of neoliberal privatization and opening to world markets and circulations. The movement of people across the globe and region for purposes of work and livelihood has expanded considerably. The People's Republic of China has 35 million migrants across the world; India

---

[29] See Benjamin E Goldsmith, "A Liberal Peace in Asia?" *Journal of Peace Research* 44, no. 1 (2007): 5–27.

[30] C.J. Wan-Ling Wee, "'We Asians?' Modernity, Visual Art Exhibitions, and East Asia," *Boundary 2* 37, no. 1 (2010): 91–126.

has 20 million, and the Philippines has 8 million. Remittances, cultural values and styles, and technical and professional knowledge from their host societies have a major impact on domestic economies and societies. As of 2001, more than 6 million migrants from Asia worked in the more advanced economies of Japan, Singapore, Taiwan, Korea, Hong Kong, and Malaysia.[31]

Elite migrants and transmigrants circulating within Asia are a novel phenomenon of these last few decades, and they have ushered in a new culture of professional Asians in the major cities. They are embedded in both knowledge and business networks and have often been trained in Western academic establishments, where they develop their professional cultural ethos and connections. These professionals are a significant element in the cultural profile of the new global and metropolitan cities in Asia, whether in Shanghai, Bangalore, Dubai, Singapore, or Hong Kong. As the workshop on "Inter-Referencing Asia," held in Dubai in 2008, points out, there is "an intensification of traffic in people, urban models, and cultural forms between Asian cities, big and small." In many ways, these cities are increasingly linked by corridors of exchange with other Asian cities, as they are with their own national or regional hinterlands. The workshop identifies these Asian—indeed, intra-Asian—cities as "extraterritorial" metropolises that are produced not only by national resources but also through a set of global and intra-Asian flows of labour, capital, and knowledge.[32] The complex known as Biopolis and its sister establishment Fusionopolis in Singapore represent classic instances of such extraterritoriality. The scientists, technicians, and professionals who work here day and often night for Asian and global biotech companies hail from every part of Asia (often with Western degrees). These gigantic mall-like complexes feature every kind of Asian eatery and omniplexes featuring

---

[31] Asian Development Bank, *Emerging Asian Regionalism,* 225; see also http://www.scalabrini.asn.au/atlas (accessed 10 August 2010).

[32] "Inter-Referencing Asia: Urban Experiments and the Art of Being Global," workshop directed by Aihwa Ong and Ananya Roy, International Conference on Inter-Asian Connections, Dubai, United Arab Emirates, 21–23 February 2008.

anime festivals, while construction and maintenance are performed by gangs of other Asian migrant labourers.

It is this new relationship between elite and working-class migration that I wish to comment on. As is well known, many Asian nations are seeking and succeeding in wooing back their talented émigrés to invest their knowledge and capital in their original homelands. Historically, this kind of migration and courtship has been exceptional. Migration over the last century and a half has largely been labour migration, mostly in plantation, mining, and infrastructure construction, but of people who have ended up in different niches in the host societies. The matrix in which this migration has taken place has been constituted by networks and institutions of global capitalism and the modern nation state, whether in its *imperialist* manifestation or its nationalist one. While, as we have seen, the relationship between the nation state and capitalism has largely been a collusive one, there has also been a tension in that relationship. To put it simply, while global capitalism has encouraged the flow of labour, nationalist states have *sought to both regulate and curb this flow by responding to a set of other interests*, including affected domestic working classes and constituencies based on racial and nationalist ideologies. Decolonizing nation states have turned out to be as limiting of immigrant populations as older imperialist nation states.

The labouring population that has both benefited and suffered most greatly from this tension between global capitalism and the nation state is the Chinese communities, first in the Americas and then in Southeast Asia. The exclusion laws against Asians in the United States until 1942 imposed strict quotas and controls on labour migrants from China. Indeed, the matrix made much immigrant labour the *exception* in the sense of Agamben—the impossible subject—necessary to labour on undesirable tasks for a pittance, but without rights, suspended between capital and the state and often between nation state jurisdictions. To be sure, much of this labour was also able to creatively manipulate their suspension between powers, as the so-called paper sons of Chinese migrants who entered the United States in large numbers during the early twentieth century show.[33]

[33] "Paper sons" were Chinese immigrants who claimed to be the sons of

What has changed in the relationship between global capitalism and the nation state? How has the globalization of recent decades changed this institutional matrix affecting migrants? One new element, as I have tried to show, is the substantially new flow of high-value workers, or professionals. Speaking impressionistically, it would seem that this is informed by the growth of what is called the knowledge economy, or knowledge-based service and production in the global economy. The fact that so much of it is Asian and circulating in the Asian region is a still more complex and interesting question. The return and transmigration of a professional and managerial stratum does signify a shift in the institutional matrix. Whereas the nation state worked to regulate the deterritorialized flows of labour, capital, and culture of capitalism even when colluding with it, now the nationalist opposition to these flows is significantly smaller, especially from the institutions of the nation state. As large states such as India and the People's Republic of China reach out to global professionals among overseas and global Chinese (*huaren, haigui*) and Indians (non-resident Indians) they create a nonterritorial, ethnic identity—as children of the Yellow Emperor or Hindutva or Bharat Pravasis—that fits with a neoliberal model of globalization and competitiveness. Until recently, this has also coincided with state withdrawal in many areas of provisioning public goods, such as education and health care.

On the other hand, labour migration, especially in seasonal and construction work, has expanded to many more societies. These labour migrants are typically sojourners who have short-term labour contracts and are prevented from assimilation into the host society. Many—such as the recent case of the Rohingas in Thailand and elsewhere—are regularly abused and exploited by local authorities and labour contractors. Moreover, unlike the previous round, there is increased sojourning by women employed as domestic workers, nurses, entertainers, and prostitutes, which, in turn, is also reshaping families across Asia. We need to focus more on the continuing power and role of the nation state to regulate and

American citizens using false papers. See Prasenjit Duara, "Between Sovereignty and Capitalism: The Historical Experiences of Migrant Chinese," in *The Global and Regional in China's Nation Formation* (London: Routledge, 2009), chap. 7

expel immigrants. The nation state continues to control the prerogative of return for them. It controls their tenure and bodies,[34] and can satisfy the constituent interests of domestic workers and nationalist interests. They can serve as an important safety valve and whipping boy.

Thus, the new order in Asia must be seen in its totality. The figure of the professional global transmigrants, their flexible citizenship, self-improvement projects, and the state's interest in utilizing them must be seen against the ground of continuing power of the restructured nation state to control and expel at the lower levels of the social hierarchy. While these Asian nations must be able to draw in and deploy migrants at the higher levels, they must be able to push out migrants at the lower levels. Thus, the new Asia does not by any means suggest the weakening of nationalism, but rather a refiguration or restructuring of the nation state to adapt to global capitalism.

WHAT KIND OF SPACE IS THIS NEW ASIA?

There are significant continuities and novelties in this space. While the nation state continues to exercise deeply rooted powers, regionally, there is no congruence or sustained effort at producing congruence between politics and culture by any state. The absence of a single dominant nation state in the region contributes significantly to this, but it is also the case that the individual nation state finds it difficult to make a coherent case for a nationalism congruent with its territorial conception. In part, this has to do with state withdrawal and growing identification with transterritorial ethnic groups such as the overseas Chinese or Indians (often at the expense of peripheries and nondominant ethnics or marginal co-nationals). Moreover, both capitalism and the nation state have transformed to the point where they celebrate heterogeneity and multiculturalism even as

---

[34] For instance, female domestic workers are required to undergo pregnancy and HIV tests every six months in Singapore. Those who are pregnant often face dismissal and deportation. See Human Rights Watch, "Maid to Order: Ending Abuses against Migrant Domestic Workers in Singapore," 2005, http://www.hrw.org/en/reports/2005/12/06/maid-order (accessed 10 August 2010).

these sociocultural factors are themselves commoditised. As the authors of the latest management fad book *Globality* suggest, for multinationals, the very idea of domestic markets has been replaced by niche markets.[35] Finally, because the nation state is much more invested in and aware of regional and global interdependence, a split has appeared in the interests and rhetoric of popular nationalism and the nation state, most evident in the People's Republic of China, but also in India, Thailand, and elsewhere. All of these factors make the political homogenization of culture or its essentialization an unnecessary and difficult process. The weakness and failure of the effort to create an ideology of Asian values in the late 1990s is a case in point.

But, as I have argued, actual interdependence has increased dramatically, and so has cultural contact. Interdependence, however, is being managed by ad hoc arrangements and specialized transnational institutions with little possibility of large-scale state-like coordination or control. In this sense, region formation in Asia is a multipath, uneven, and pluralistic development that is significantly different from European regionalism. Moreover, the region has no external limits or territorial boundaries and does not seek to homogenize itself within. Individual nations, economic, regulatory, cultural entities, and non-governmental organizations have multiple links beyond the core, and when a country beyond the core arrives at the threshold of a sufficiently dense set of interactions and dependencies with it, it may brought within the region's frameworks of governance. Conceivably, this could include even regions outside the cartographic scope of Asia, say, for instance, South Africa. At least this has been the pattern in recent years.

Culturally, this plurality indicates a move away from an essentialist identity formation even when different Asians consume common cultural goods. Thus, consuming Korean television serials with the voracious appetite that has been revealed in East and Southeast Asia does not end up transforming an identity from, say, Vietnamese or Taiwanese to Korean.

---

[35] Harold Sirkin, James Hemerling, and Arindam Bhattacharya, *Globality: Competing with Everyone from Everywhere for Everything* (New York: Business Plus, 2008).

Rather, as Chua Beng Huat has pointed out, it requires the consumer to "transcend his or her grounded nationality to forge abstract identification with the foreign characters on screen, a foreignness that is, in turn, potentially reabsorbed into an idea of (East) 'Asia.'"[36] Indeed, I am not sure that this foreignness even need be reabsorbed. The reception of the Asian cultural product can remain a site of circulation and interaction, one that implicitly questions pure identity in the recognition of multiple connections and interdependence. It can remain without the potential of absorption into another political project of nationalism or another grand Othering process.

In a more literary language, Gayatri Chakravorty Spivak has described a similar ideal: "To combat the desire for an origin in a name, I propose to deal with 'Asia' as the instrument of altered citation: an iteration. Indeed, the possibility of the desire for a singular origin is in its iterability." She points to different "histories, languages, and idioms 'that come forth' each time we try to add an 's' to the wish for a unified originary name".[37] Tagore would probably agree with Spivak. But identities are designed to emphasize exclusivity; presumably, that is their nature. Efforts to bridge differences have historically been the loser in the era of identitarian politics heralded by the nation state and nationalism. In addition to founding the call for heterogeneity and plurality of homelands on textual, imaginative, and psychological grounds, I wish to emphasize our interdependence as necessary for our survival and even for individual flourishing. We *need* to recognize our interdependence and foster transnational consciousness in our education and cultural institutions, not *at* the cost but *for* the cost of our national attachments.

In an earlier work, I argued that in pre-nationalist societies, political forces such as imperial or feudal states, did not seek to dominate every aspect of a person's identity. These societies were characterized by soft boundaries, where individual community difference (say, in diet or belief in deities) would not prevent large-scale and un-self-conscious

[36] Beng-huat Chua, "Conceptualizing an East Asian Popular Culture," *Inter-Asian Cultural Studies* 5, no. 2 (August 2004): 200-21.

[37] Gayatri Chakravorty Spivak, *Other Asias* (Oxford: Blackwell, 2008), 217, 220.

borrowing in other respects. Modern nationalisms sought precisely to create hard boundaries between communities by privileging a defining characteristic of community (say language) as constitutive of the self in a self-conscious way that often developed intolerance for the non-national Other.[38] The Asian maritime networks of the precolonial era exemplified such a framework. This long-distance trade involved a wide variety of merchant communities at different points who did not speak the same languages or trade in the same currencies. Yet as Janet Abu-Lughod says, goods were transferred, prices set, exchange rates agreed upon, contracts contracted, credit extended, partnerships formed, records kept, and agreements honoured. Trade was contained "within the interstices of a larger collaboration in which goods and merchants from many places were intermingled on each others' ships and where unwritten rules of reciprocity assured general compliance. This system was not decisively challenged until the sixteenth century, when the Portuguese men-of-war violated all the rules of the game."[39]

I am by no means arguing that we return—or can return—to the pre-national mode of identities; rather, I want to see whether the nationalist congruence between state and culture exemplified by the hard boundary may have represented a long twentieth-century moment. Certainly, the present regional nexus resembles the earlier Asian maritime networks in terms of this non-congruence. Although the actual products flowing through the Asian maritime networks were miniscule compared to today's figures, the cultural flows they enabled—packaged in Hinduism, Buddhism, Confucianism, Daoism, and Islam—were nothing short of world transforming. They created interlinked cultural universes, however, that were rarely accompanied by the kind of political domination that became hegemonic from the nineteenth century. To be sure, today's cultural identities are shaped by circulations of culture, knowledge, technology, goods, services, and finance that are dizzying in their velocity, while also becoming deeply commodified or consumerist. Nonetheless, the older

---

[38] Prasenjit Duara, *Rescuing History from the Nation: Questioning Narratives of Modern China* (Chicago: University of Chicago Press, 1995), chap. 2.

[39] Abu-Lughod, "The World System in the Thirteenth Century," 11.

Asian models of cultural circulation without state domination of identity present us with a historical resource to explore new possibilities.

But the two dimensions of migration remind us that regional formation is taking place under capitalist liberalization and state restructuring. While this favours the emergence of a professional and capitalist Asian community with its cultural openness and ability to forge multiple linkages and new cultures from their encounter, the power of the nation state remains entrenched in relation to the movement—especially the transnational movement—of labour. The neoliberal circumstances under which regional formation is taking place can easily develop the concept of Asia for the rich and their representatives who attend to financial flows, knowledge economies, and corporatization, while containing or displacing the poor and privatizing public goods. It is well established that while globalization produces wealth, it also creates stratification and a deeper gulf between the rich and the poor. Does regionalism under these circumstances do the same? The verdict is not fully out on this, but it is clear that regionalism possesses a greater ability to bring states and other political actors together to address common problems and achieve common goals, if only because of the more limited scale and recognizable commonality of problems. Of course, a time such as the economic crisis of the present will represent a test for these nation states. Will they withdraw to domestic protectionism and expel foreign elements or will they seek common solutions? In what degree will they engage in each? Has the expansion of regional interests and interdependence only yielded state-led and corporate modes of connecting and coordinating? If so, it will not be easy to prevent the entrenchment of the Asian elite *versus* the poor. We need to draw attention and encourage civil society organizations—the NGOs that have mushroomed in most Asian societies over the last few decades—to develop their linkages and guard the interests of the region as a whole.

The Idea of Asia and Its Ambiguities

WANG HUI

Prasenjit Duara's "Asia Redux: Conceptualizing a Region for Our Times" is a rich and inspiring paper. The distinction between the concept of region and the concept of regionalization shows the author's historical approach. Asia as a region in the nineteenth and twentieth centuries was the result of imperial regionalism and the anti-imperialist regionalization project. The question of Asian "modernity" must eventually deal with the relationships both between Asia and European colonialism and between Asia and modern capitalism. A lot of research has shown Asia as a region from a long historical perspective, but most can be thought of as a modern construction of the early history of Asia in light of imperial or anti-imperialist projects in the nineteenth and twentieth centuries.

For example, as early as the 1940s, Miyazaki Ichisada began to explore the "birth of Song dynasty capitalism" through the study of wide-ranging historical transportation links, believing firmly that the study of "the development of modernity after the Song has brought us to the point of needing to reflect on modern Western history in terms of the development of modern East Asian history."[1] That his theory of "East Asian modernity" overlapped with the Japanese idea of a "Greater East Asia" does not obscure the insight inhering in Miyazaki's observations. He saw that from the perspective of world history, the digging of the Grand Canal, urban migration, the ability of the circulation of commodities such as spices and tea to connect European and Asian trade networks, and the promotion of artistic and cultural exchange between Europe and Asia enabled by the expansion of the Mongolian empire not only changed the internal relations in Chinese and Asian societies, but also connected Europe and

[1] Miyazaki Ichisada, "Dongyangde jinshi" [East Asian Modernity], *Riben xuezhe,* 1: 240.

Asia by land and sea.[2] If the political, economic, and cultural features of "Asian modernity" appeared as early as the tenth or eleventh centuries, was the historical development of these two worlds merely parallel, or more closely linked?

Andre Gunder Frank responded to this question by noting that Asia and Europe were already profoundly tied together by the thirteenth or fourteenth centuries, and as a result, any discussion of the birth of modernity must proceed on the assumption of a world system characterized by such relations.[3] The significance of communication is not the mere bundling together of two worlds; it is more like two gears connected by a belt: when one turns, the other must turn as well. So a logical conclusion is that,

> If history were only European the Industrial Revolution would never have eventuated, because it was not merely a matter of mechanization but a matter of the whole social structure. The rise of the petit-bourgeoisie was a necessary precondition for the Industrial Revolution, and it also required the capital accumulated through trade with East Asia. Making the machines work required not just motive power but also cotton as raw material and markets into which to sell the finished products, both of which were in fact

[2] Ichisada, "Dongyangde jinshi", in *Selected Translations of Japanese Scholars' Research on Chinese History,* vol. 1 (Beijing: Zhonghuashuju, 1993), 163, 166.

[3] Frank points out that both the European population and European capitalism within the world economy have grown steadily since 1400, and that this process is consistent with the East's decline since around 1800. European countries used the silver they acquired from their colonies in the Americas to buy their way into Asian markets that were expanding at the time. For Europe, the commercial and political mechanisms for this Asian market were unique and effective from the perspective of the worldwide economy. Just as Asia began to decline, Western countries became rising industrial economies through the mechanisms of import and export. In this sense, modern European capitalism resulted both from changes in relations of production within European societies and out of its relationship with Asia. See Andre Gunder Frank, *ReOrient: Global Economy in the Asian Age* (Berkeley and Los Angeles: University of California Press, 1998).

> supplied by East Asia. Lacking interaction with East Asia, in other words, the Industrial Revolution probably would not have taken place.[4]

Miyazaki's research centres mainly on Chinese history proper, and his writings on the intercourse between Asia and Europe are thin. Frank's research, on the other hand, is economistic and trade centred, lacking convincing explanations of the internal dynamics of European history and the capitalism that these dynamics produced. In their structured narratives based on a maritime world, wars, contingent events, and other historical factors are necessarily pushed into the background. Both accounts, however, from their different perspectives provide us with the possibility to create new narratives of "world history."

In such an interactive historical narrative, then, the efficacy of the idea of Asia diminishes, as it is neither a self-contained entity nor a set of self-contained relations; it is neither the beginning nor the end of a linear world history. It would be better to say that this "Asia"—neither starting point nor end, neither self-sufficient subject nor subordinate object—provides the moment to reconstruct "world history." If we need to rectify mistakes in theories of "Asia," we must also reexamine the notion of Europe. As we correct the errors in the idea of Asia, we must also re-examine the idea of Europe. To borrow Lenin's phrasing, we should ask, where does this advanced Europe come from, after all? What sort of historical relations have resulted in Asia's backwardness? Historical relations internal to societies are important, but in the historical long run, how should we appraise the effects of ever-extending interregional relations on a society's internal transformation? If the discourse on Asia continues to be based on notions of Europe that are taken as self-evident, and the motive forces that gave rise to the concept of Europe are not re-understood through a penetrating review of European historical development, this discourse will not be able to overcome its lack of clarity.

The accounts of Asia discussed here demonstrate not so much Asia's autonomy as the ambiguities and contradictions in the idea of Asia itself: the idea is at once colonialist and anticolonialist, conservative and

---

4 Ichisada, "Dongyangde jinshi," in *Selected Translations*, 236–38.

revolutionary, nationalist and internationalist, originating in Europe and, alternatively, shaping Europe's image of itself. It is closely related to issues of both nation state and empire, a notion of a civilization seen as the opposite of the European, and a geographic category established through geopolitics. I believe that as we examine the political, economic, and cultural autonomy of Asia, we must take seriously the derivativeness, ambiguity, and inconsistency that were intertwined with the history of its advent—these are products of specific historical relationships, and it is only from these relationships that they can be transcended or overcome.

From here, let me summarise some points of thought in my earlier work, "The Politics of Imagining Asia" (*Inter-Asia Cultural Studies* 8, no. 1 [March 2007]: 1–33) about the idea of Asia. First, the idea of Asia was always closely related to issues of "modernity" and capitalism, and at the core of the question of "modernity" lay the development of the relationship between nation state and market. The tension in the notion of Asia between nationalism and supra-nationalism is closely related to the reliance of capitalist markets on both the state and interstate relations. Because discussion of Asia is rooted in such issues as the nation state and capitalism, the full diversity of historical relations among Asian societies, institutional forms, customs, and cultural patterns comes to be understood only through the narrative of "modernity," and analysis of values, institutions, and rituals independent of that narrative has either been suppressed or marginalized. It is in this sense that, even as we challenge the Eurocentric historical narrative, how we go about unearthing these suppressed historical legacies—values, institutions, rituals, and economic relations—and rethinking European "world history" become key tasks.

Second, at this point, the nation state is still emphatically the main force behind advancing regional relations within Asia, with the following manifestations: (1) regional relations are the extension of state relations: whether we are talking about the Asian Forum promoted by Malaysia, or the East Asian Network advocated by South Korea, or regional organizations such as ASEAN or the Shanghai Six, all of these are interstate relationships formed along the axis of developing economic association or state security collaboration. (2) Asian sovereignty has yet to be fully established: the standoffs on the Korean peninsula and the Taiwan Straits and the incomplete sovereignty of postwar Japan all illustrate that the nationalism set in motion in the nineteenth century still determines, to a large extent, power relations in East Asia. (3) Because the new discourse on Asia tends to be directed at forming protective and constructive regional networks against the unilateral dominance and turbulence brought about by globalization, the national question still lies at the centre of the Asian question. Imagining Asia often appeals to an ambiguous Asian identity, but if we examine the premises underlying the institutions and principles of this idea, the nation state emerges as the political structure needing to be overcome. So, how to deal in the present with the legacy of national liberation movements (respect for sovereignty, equality, mutual trust, and the like) and traditional regional relations is still a question demanding the most serious consideration.

Third, and closely related to the first two questions, the dominance of the nation state in Asian imaginaries arose from the empire/nation state binary created in modern Europe. The historical import of this binary is that the nation state is the only modern political form and the most important premise for the development of capitalism. The binary, however, not only oversimplifies the diversity of political and economic relations subsumed under the category of empire, but also underestimates the internal diversity within individual nation states.

Modern Asian imaginaries are based mainly on interstate relations and seldom deal with Asia's complex ethnicities, regional communications and forms of interaction that are conventionally grouped under the category of empire—for example, trans-state tribute networks, migration patterns, and the like. The question is this: in an era in which the nation state has become the dominant political structure, will the traditional Asian experiences of various types of communication, coexistence, and institutions provide possibilities for overcoming the internal and external dilemmas brought about by the nation state system?

Fourth, the category of an Asian totality was established in contradistinction to Europe, and it encompasses heterogeneous cultures, religions, and other social elements. Whether from the perspective of historical traditions or contemporary institutions, Asia lacks the conditions for creating a European Union-style superstate. Buddhism, Judaism, Christianity, Hinduism, Islam, Sikhism, Zoroastrianism, Daoism, and Confucianism all originated on this continent we call Asia, which represents three-fifths of the world's landmass and contains more than half of the world's population; thus, any attempt to characterise Asia as a unitary culture is not plausible. The idea of Confucian Asia cannot account even for China itself, and even if we reduce the idea of Asia only to East Asia, we cannot escape the region's cultural heterogeneity. Any new imagining of Asia must combine a vision of cultural and political diversity with regional political and economic structures. A high degree of cultural heterogeneity does not mean that Asia cannot form definite regional structures; it merely reminds us that any such structure must have a high degree of flexibility and pluralism. Two possible directions for imagining Asia are, therefore, (1) to draw on the institutional experiences of Asian cultural coexistence in order to develop new models that will allow different cultures, religions, and peoples to get along on equal terms within the context of the nation state and the Asian region; and (2) to form multilayered, open social organizations and networks linked through regional connections to coordinate economic development, mitigate conflicts of interest, and diminish the dangers inhering in the nation state system.

Fifth, Asia has historically longstanding and unbreakable religious, trade, cultural, military, and political ties to Europe, Africa, and the Americas, so to describe Asia on the model of or to assume it to be something like an enlarged nation state is equally inappropriate. The idea of Asia has never been purely self-delimited, but rather is the product of interaction with other regions; the critique of Eurocentrism is not an affirmation of Asiacentrism, but rather an attempt to eradicate a logic dominated by egocentrism, exclusivity, and expansionism. In this sense, discerning the disorder and pluralism within the "new empire" and breaking down the self-evident notion of Europe are not only important preconditions for reconstructing the ideas of Asia and Europe, but also the path required to break out of the "new imperial logic."

Sixth, if the excavation of Asia's cultural potential is also a critique of Western-centrism, then the reconstruction of the idea of Asia also constitutes defiance of the colonial, interfering, and dominating forces that have divided Asia. The commonality of Asian imaginaries partly derives from subordinate status under Western colonialism, during the Cold War, and in the current global order, and also rises out of Asian movements for national self-determination, socialism, and colonial liberation. If we fail to acknowledge these historical conditions and movements, we will not be able to understand the implications of modernity for Asia or the sources of its division and war perils. People regard the fall of the Berlin Wall and the dissolution of the Soviet Union and the Eastern European socialist bloc as the end of the "Cold War," but in Asia, the structure of the Cold War has, to a large extent, been preserved and has developed new derivative forms under new historical conditions. Contemporary discussions of the question of Asia, however, are carried out either by state actors or intellectual elites, and the numerous Asian social movements—whether of workers, students, peasants, or women—are indifferent to it. This stands in sharp contrast to the tempestuous surge of Asian national liberation in the twentieth century. If it can be said that the socialist and national liberation movements of the twentieth century have drawn to a close, their fragmentary remains can still be a vital source for stimulating new ways of imagining Asia.

By way of conclusion, let me emphasise once again what I have been attempting to convey: the issue of Asia is not simply an Asian issue, but rather a matter of "world history." Reconsidering "Asian history" is at once to reconstruct nineteenth-century European "world history," and an effort to break free of the twenty-first-century "new imperial" order and its associated logic.

The Intricacies of Premodern Asian Connections

TANSEN SEN

In his essay "Asia Redux: Conceptualizing a Region for Our Times," Prasenjit Duara has aptly underscored the importance of comprehending the patterns of interactions and connectivities among Asian societies during the precolonial period. The following comments will reaffirm most of his contentions, but also will problematise the issue, especially in regard to some of the neglected topics and the conceptualization of the premodern interactions.

I will address three issues. First, Duara's paper emphasizes Asian interactions, mostly through the maritime channels, starting sometime in the thirteenth or fourteenth century. He also mentions, albeit briefly, that these contacts extend further back in history. The first section of my comments will elaborate on these pre-thirteenth-century linkages in order to demonstrate that they contributed significantly to the formation of later networks of exchange. I will highlight the role played by the intermediary states and peoples in linking various parts of Asia during the first millennium of the common era. The current emphasis on premodern India and China often obscures the important contributions made by these intermediary states and people.

Second, I will argue that conflicts and warfare were also important elements of cross-cultural interactions in precolonial Asia. These often involved military confrontations and political aspirations to control strategic passes, straits, and territories. Thus, looking back into the past does not necessarily provide us with a model for peace and harmony that can be replicated in contemporary political discourse, as politicians from some Asian countries have tried to do.

The final section of my comments will attempt to conceptualize the intricacies of premodern intra-Asian interactions. I will suggest that these interactions must be conceived within the larger context of Afro-Eurasian networks, as well as through a focus on subregional linkages. The use of the word "Asia," in my opinion, does not reflect the breadth of premodern interactions or the intricate exchanges that took place within the subregions of the Asian continent.

INTERMEDIARIES AND THE AFRO-EURASIAN NETWORKS

The major ports and urban centers of Asia were linked with each other by at least the first century CE. The key to the creation of these linkages (and the urban centres themselves) was the emergence of trading networks, consisting of both overland and maritime routes. Funan and the Kushana empire were important intermediaries in these networks. These two polities also played a crucial role in the transmission of Buddhist ideas from South to East Asia. Equally important were the itinerant merchants, proselytizers, artisans, nomads, and other travellers belonging to diverse ethnic groups who moved from one place to another, creating new networks and transmitting ideas and knowledge among societies far-flung from each other.

Originating from complex migratory patterns and military conflicts, the Kushanas, a branch of the Central Asiatic group known to the Chinese as Yuezhi, in the first century CE established one of the most influential empires in Asia. The empire reached its peak during the second century CE under Kanishka, whose power seems to have extended to the eastern coastal regions of ancient India. Consequently, the oasis states around the Taklamakan desert in eastern Central Asia and the Bay of Bengal were linked through networks of trade routes and cultural exchanges.[1] It was during this time that Buddhism makes its appearance in China, brought, it seems, by the Indo-Scythian and Indo-Parthian traders who travelled these trading networks.[2]

---

[1] B.N. Mukherjee, *Kushana Studies: New Perspectives* (Kolkata: Firma KLM, 2004).

[2] Xinru Liu, *Ancient India and Ancient China: Trade and Religious Exchanges, AD 1–600* (New Delhi: Oxford University Press, 1988).

It must be noted, however, that the overland paths rimming the Taklamakan desert into China and the maritime routes that connected the coastal regions of ancient India and China existed prior to the establishment of the Kushana empire. Significant numbers of trade goods, including beads and glass, reached present-day Malaysia, Cambodia, Vietnam, and Thailand during the last two centuries BCE.[3] These goods became elements of the regional trading networks that connected the islands of Sumatra and Java, mainland Southeast Asia, and the southwestern region of China. At the same time, because some of these commodities originated in the Mediterranean region, these trade routes also intersected with networks that linked southern India to the Roman Empire. To the east, the networks centred in Southeast Asia extended to Hepu, in today's Guangxi Province in China, where similar international trade commodities are found in Western Han graves.[4]

The emergence of Funan, also in the first century CE in present-day Cambodia and Vietnam was closely associated with the growth of interregional and intraregional trade and the development of hinterland agriculture.[5] Commercial specialists from the Indian subcontinent, Sogdian horse traders, and diplomats from Chinese kingdoms also started frequenting the Southeast Asian kingdom. Indic cultural elements, especially those from the brahmanical and Buddhist traditions, started influencing Southeast Asian societies during this period, leading to what some scholars have called the "Indianization" of the region.[6] These cultural exchanges, similar to the trading interactions, extended beyond

---

[3] Bérénice Bellina and Ian Glover, "The Archaeology of Early Contact with India and the Mediterranean World, from the Fourth Century BC to the Fourth Century AD", in *Southeast Asia: From Prehistory to History,* edited by Ian Glover and Peter Bellwood (New York: RoutledgeCurzon, 2004), 68-88.

[4] Gan Fuxi, "The Silk Road and Ancient Chinese Glass," in *Ancient Glass Research along the Silk Road,* edited by Gan Fuxi, Robert H. Brill, and Tian Shouyun (Hackensack, N.J.: World Scientific, 2009), 41-108.

[5] Pierre-Yves Manguin, "The Archaeology of Early Maritime Polities of Southeast Asia," in *Southeast Asia: From Prehistory to History,* edited by Ian Glover and Peter Bellwood (New York: Routledge, 2004), 282–313.

[6] R.C. Majumdar, *Hindu Colonies in the Far East* (Calcutta: Firma KLM, 1963);

the Southeast Asian region. They were part of the wider networks that incorporated several overland and maritime routes. This is best illustrated in the journey of the Chinese monk Faxian, who travelled from China to the Indian subcontinent through Central Asia in the fifth century but returned by the maritime route. Also evident from his trip is the integrated nature of the trading and cultural networks, within which monks and itinerant merchants supported each other on long-distance voyages.[7]

The travels of Buddhist monks and long-distance traders also reveal that Central and Southeast Asia were more than mere conduits for the movement of people and goods. Not only did these areas supply important commodities such as horses from Central Asia and spices originating in Southeast Asia to the stream of international commerce, they also were places of cross-regional learning and education. The Sriwijayan kingdom, the successor to Funan, attracted Buddhist monks from both India and China. The Chinese monk Yijing and the Indian Atisa are two leading examples of Buddhists who studied in Sriwijaya before proceeding to their respective destinations, Yijing to Nalanda and Atisa eventually to Tibet.[8] A similar role was played by the Central Asian oasis states, where monks from China went to learn about Buddhism, and where, in the later periods, Indian monks resided to learn Chinese.

Finally, the contributions made by Persians and Arabs in linking the markets of Asia to those in Africa and Europe must be recognized. In fact, India and China would have had limited impact beyond eastern continental Asia without the Persian and Arab traders and their ships and caravans. People from the Persian Gulf were active along the overland and maritime networks from at least the early first millennium CE.[9] While some were

---

and G. Coedès, *The Indianised States of Southeast Asia* (Honolulu: East-West Center Press, 1968).

[7] Tansen Sen, *Buddhism, Diplomacy, and Trade: The Realignment of Sino-Indian Relations, 600–1400* (Honolulu: University of Hawaii Press, 2003).

[8] John Miksic, "The Hindu-Buddhist Divide in Premodern Southeast Asia," Working paper no. 1, Nalanda-Sriwijaya Centre 2010, http://www.iseas.edu.sg/nsc/publications_working_paper_series.htm (accessed 12 August 2010).

[9] J. T. Reinaud, *Relation des voyages faits par les Arabes et les Persans dans l'Inde*

involved in the transmission of religious ideas, including Buddhism and Manichaeism, others traded in commodities within the vast Afro-Eurasian networks. The role of the Persians and Arabs increased significantly in the post-seventh-century period, when they became instrumental in the transmission of Islam and the growth of maritime trade in the Indian Ocean. Indeed, the rise of China and India during the premodern period owes much to these intermediaries, who sustained cross-continental commercial activity from Song China to Spain. And, as is apparent from the foregoing discussion, these networks of exchange from eastern Asia to the Mediterranean were all fairly well established by the thirteenth century. The interactions during the subsequent periods, including the voyages of Zheng He and the trading activities of the European commercial enterprises, often followed many of these ancient pathways.

MILITARY SKIRMISHES AND REGIME CHANGES

Although new and seminal research on military conflicts in premodern Asia has appeared in recent years,[10] studies on "Asian" interactions and exchanges often seem to suggest that the exchanges were of a peaceful, harmonious, and nonconfrontational nature before the colonial period. Even when conflicts and warfare are mentioned, they are mostly ascribed to the nomadic tribes. Warfare and expansionist actions of the settled empires abound in the history of interactions among Asian societies. Some of these expansionist activities had a significant impact on cultural exchanges, trading interactions, and the balance of power in specific regions. The opening of the so-called Silk Road in the second century BCE, for example, was related to the confrontation between the Western Han court in China and the Xiongnu confederation in Central Asia. Later, the

et à la Chine dans le IXe sièle de l'èrechrétienne [Discussion of Arab and Persian voyages in India and China in the ninth century of the Christian Era], 2 vols. (Paris: l'Imprimerie Royale, 1845).

10 See, e.g., Nicola Di Cosmo, *Ancient China and Its Enemies: The Rise of Nomadic Power in East Asian History* (Cambridge: Cambridge University Press, 2002).

Mongol empire, which is applauded for the intra-Eurasian connections it facilitated,[11] also resulted from conquests and warfare.

Here I would like to provide some examples of how polities in India and China attempted to exert power over the maritime trading networks, sometimes resulting in naval confrontations. The first case relates to the Chola naval expedition against the Sriwijayan kingdom in Southeast Asia in 1025. The second example concerns the Ming court's dominance of the Indian Ocean maritime networks during the early fifteenth century. These two examples suggest that even before the arrival of the Portuguese, the British, and other European powers, Asian kingdoms vied with each other to control key locations on the Asian maritime trading routes. The display of military might, the commercial interests of merchant groups, cross-cultural diplomacy, and the involvement of foreign powers in internal politics and regional conflicts are all evident from these two episodes.

The eleventh to the twelfth century was one of the most vibrant periods in the history of premodern interactions in Asia. Extensive interregional and intraregional commercial networks of Muslim traders had linked most of Afro-Eurasia; the Song court in China had instituted economic measures that nurtured the vast networks that connected the three continents; and while traders and rulers from the Chola and Sriwijayan kingdoms actively participated in the transit trade through the maritime networks, the Uighurs, Khitans, and Jurchens did the same for the overland routes. By this time, external trade had become closely linked to the internal economies of many Asian kingdoms. A case in point is Song China, which became dependent on profits from maritime trade for its fiscal needs. It was for this reason that the Song court also commercialized the tribute system. For the first time in Chinese history, foreign tribute carriers were allowed to legally conduct trade and encouraged to offer goods that had commercial value, many of which the court sold in local markets to add to its coffers.[12]

---

[11] Janet L. Abu-Lughod, *Before European Hegemony: The World System* A.D. *1250–1350* (New York: Oxford University Press, 1989).

[12] Robert Hartwell, "The Imperial Treasuries: Finances and Power in Song China," *Bulletin of Sung-Yüan Studies* 20 (1988): 18–89; and Hartwell, "Foreign

The commercialization of the tribute system and the encouragement of foreign trade by the Song court led to intense competition among individual merchants and states that were in a position to profit from the trading activity that stretched from the ports in Song China to the Middle East. The naval offensive by the Cholas against the Sriwijayan kingdom in 1025 seems to have stemmed from the desire to access Song markets. By the early tenth century, the Chola and the Sriwijayan polities had emerged as important transit centres in maritime commerce, with efficient port facilities and powerful naval forces. In fact, both kingdoms frequently used their navies to control key sections of the maritime route. While the Cholas dominated the Bay of Bengal segment, the Sriwijayans controlled the Straits of Malacca and the South China Sea region.

On several occasions, the Sriwijayans tried to hinder direct diplomatic and commercial links between Song China and the southern coastal regions of India. Envoys from Sriwijaya to the Song court seem to have been responsible for creating the perception in China that the Sriwijayans had subjugated the Chola kingdom, and therefore it was they who were deserving of trading privileges in China. In fact, on one occasion, the Sriwijayan envoys appeared at the Song court as representatives of the Chola court.[13] The success of the Chola naval expedition, the first of its kind in the history of Indian Ocean interactions, is reflected not only in the sudden decline in the Sriwijayan tributary missions to the Song court, but also in the local legends found in the Malay annals known as *Serajah Melayu*, which suggests a marriage alliance between the Cholas and the Sriwijayans.[14]

Trade, Monetary Policy and Chinese 'Mercantilism,'" in *Collected Studies on Sung History Dedicated to James T.C. Liu in Celebration of his Seventieth Birthday*, edited by Kinugawa Tsuyoshi (Kyoto: Dohosha, 1989), 453–88.

[13] Tansen Sen, "The Military Campaigns of Rajendra Chola and the Chola-Srivijaya-China Triangle," in *Nagapattinam to Suvarnadwipa: Reflections on the Chola Naval Expeditions to Southeast Asia*, edited by Hermann Kulke, K. Kesavapany and Vijay Sakhuja (Singapore: Institute of Southeast Asian Studies, 2009), 61–75.

[14] George Spencer, *The Politics of Expansion: The Chola Conquest of Sri Lanka and Sri Vijaya* (Madras: New Era, 1983).

Almost four centuries later, Ming China emerged as the most dominant naval power in Asia. The political goals, both symbolic and pragmatic, of the Zheng He voyages have been overshadowed by the representation that these were missions of peace and diplomacy. However, a detailed study of the reasons for launching these voyages and of the actions of Zheng He and his entourage reveals that the Ming court exerted considerable power in the Indian Ocean through these missions, capturing foreign rulers, engaging in conflict resolution, and even attempting to change the balance of power in regions far from the coastal regions of Ming China.

The first voyage in 1405 may have been launched to meet the immediate political goals of the Ming court. One of the leading arguments is that the Yongle emperor (r. 1402–24) dispatched Zheng He to find the deposed ruler Jianwen (r. 1398–1402). Also put forth as a possibility is the plan to investigate Tamerlane's (r. 1336–1405) impending attack on Ming China. A third reason seems to be Yongle's interest in asserting his naval supremacy, at the same time his army invaded Vietnam and Mongolia, to extract the traditional-style tributary missions from the maritime kingdoms.[15]

Whatever Zheng He's initial orders from Yongle may have been, the famous admiral made prudent use of the large numbers of troops and naval vessels that accompanied his armada. Already during his first trip, he had used this naval might to defeat and capture the so-called pirate Chen Zuyi in Palembang. Although Ming sources, and many modern scholars, portray this event as a major contribution of Zheng He in stopping the menace of piracy in the Straits of Malacca, these one-sided and uncorroborated Chinese sources must be used with caution. Similarly, the Ming report that Zheng He in 1415 captured Sekandar, the king of Sumudera (in northern Sumatra), at the "request" of the deposed ruler Zain al-'Abidin, who was recognized by the Ming court, cannot be taken as the only possible explanation. Before his capture of Sekandar, Zheng He, in 1410, as a "self-defense" measure, had also defeated and captured the ruler of Sri Lanka called Alakeshwara. And starting from his first trip, Zheng He may have been involved in the conflict between Calicut and

---

[15] Edward L. Dreyer, *Zheng He: China and the Oceans in the Early Ming Dynasty, 1405–1433* (New York: Pearson Longman, 2007).

Cochin, an engagement that seems to have eventually resulted in his death in the area in 1433.

The regions where Zheng He intervened militarily were strategic locations on the maritime networks previously controlled by the Sriwijayans and Cholas. Even in the areas that Zheng He did not personally visit, his aides inserted themselves into local conflicts. In the discord between the Bengal Sultanate and the neighbouring Jaunpur, for example, ships and troops belonging to Zheng He's armada visited the courts of the two Indian kingdoms and brokered a peaceful settlement.[16]

While Zheng He does not seem to have stationed his troops or established any long-term fortifications in these regions, it is clear that his armada wielded enormous power from the southern coastal region of China to the Malabar coast of India. Where necessary, Zheng He displayed this power with military force. Clearly, the view that these unprecedented maritime voyages signified the peaceful diplomatic enterprise of the Ming court must be subject to further scrutiny. They may not rise to the level of "proto-colonialism," as Geoffrey Wade has proposed in his reexamination,[17] but the Chola expedition and the Zheng He missions are indicative of Asian powers employing naval supremacy and controlling, through military force, key regions of the Indian Ocean before the arrival of the Europeans.

CONCEPTUALIZING PREMODERN INTERACTIONS IN ASIA

Interactions among Asian societies before the sixteenth century were more complex than can be represented in the examples presented here. They involved various kinds of knowledge sharing, the transfer of technologies, the establishment of diasporic networks, and religious and cultural transmissions. In the nineteenth and twentieth centuries, these interactions were "rediscovered" by Asian intellectuals living under colonial

[16] Tansen Sen, "The Formation of Chinese Maritime Networks to Southern Asia, 1200–1450", *Journal of the Economic and Social History of the Orient* 49, no. 4 (2006): 421–53.

[17] Geoffrey Wade, "The Zheng He Voyages: A Reassessment," *Journal of the Malaysian Branch of the Royal Asiatic Society* 78, no. 1 (2005): 37–58.

rule. This rediscovery was influenced by the new ideas of nationalism and pan-Asianism, where Asia was presented as "one" and united through, as Okakura suggested,[18] the confluence of Indian and Chinese civilizations. Within this context, several scholars in India and China started highlighting their respective precolonial legacies within a broader and culturally constructed Asia. In India, the Greater India Society promoted the idea of Indianization of Southeast Asia. In China, on the other hand, Liang Qichao and others portrayed Zheng He as the great navigator and diplomat of Asia. Unfortunately, such embellished narratives of premodern Asian history continue to have an impact on modern scholarship. Asia is emphasised as an exceptional and peaceful zone of premodern cross-cultural interactions, with India and China having salient and critical roles in these exchanges. This emphasis, however, obscures several key elements of premodern interactions.

First, the interactions and exchanges within Asia were often intimately linked to regions outside the continent, a point that Duara makes several times in his paper. From the commerce between Indus and Egypt during the second millennium BCE to the silk, porcelain, and spice trade of the first and second millennium CE, the networks of exchange extended to the continents of Asia, Africa, and Europe. These commercial exchanges indicate that the traders in Asia were as dependent on the markets outside the continent as the commercial activities elsewhere were on the markets in Asia. The travels and expeditions of many individuals are also indicative of these wider connections. Alexander the Great, Marco Polo, and Ibn Battuta are just a few examples of people who used the Afro-Eurasian networks. Even Zheng He's voyages reached beyond the Asian continent to the shores of Africa.

Second, parallel to these wider, cross-continental networks of exchanges, there were also smaller, more exclusive networks that linked only specific regions of the Asian continent. This included the Bay of Bengal network that connected Sri Lanka, the eastern coastal region of the Indian Subcontinent, Burma, and parts of Southeast Asia. The Theravada

[18] Okakura Kakuzo, *The Ideals of the East with Special Reference to the Arts of Japan* (London: John Murray, 1903).

Buddhism linkages are perhaps one of the most prominent features of this network. Similar subregional networks also existed in the East China Sea, in the Mongolian Steppe region, and elsewhere.

Third, the emphasis on India and China, both of which are problematic designations in the premodern context, diminishes the role of intermediary states and people who played a critical role in connecting the regions of Asia. These places and people not only facilitated trade between the Indian subcontinent and successive Chinese polities, but also contributed to the exchange of ideas and technologies. Similarly, Arab and Persian traders were critical players in linking the markets of India and China to those in the Middle East and Europe. The rise of India and China cannot be understood, nor perhaps could it have taken place, without the active participation of these intermediaries.

Fourth, conflicts and warfare also have to be accounted for in the study of premodern Afro-Eurasian interactions. While it is true that commercial and cultural exchanges during the premodern period mostly took place without a hegemonic power, there were times when states took punitive actions to express their desire to control or profit from cross-regional interactions. Sometimes these activities were conducive to the interactions and led to their intensification, and at other times, they hindered and prevented long-distance travel and trade. Also important to note are the instances when large states attempted to intervene in smaller networks of exchange or tried to prevent the rise of an alternate port or emporium of trade. In the second century BCE, the Western Han court, for example, tried to intercede in the trading activity taking place in the Yunnan–Burma–India region just to find an alternate route to Central Asia and confront their military rivals the Xiongnus. The state of Calicut in the Malabar coast, on the other hand, may have tried to prevent the rise of the nearby Cochin as an alternate port of international commerce in the fifteenth century CE. This was a conflict in which Zheng He, a representative from faraway Ming China, seems to have become involved and lost his life.

Asia was neither the core nor a world to itself during premodern times. Just as the current "rise" or "reemergence" of Asia cannot be understand without the global context and exclusive of the markets and economies elsewhere in the world, the intensive commercial and cultural exchanges within the Asian continent during premodern times should not be looked at only through a pan-Asian prism. The interactions could also transcend the Asian continent, or could be limited to a subregion. Now, following the control and domination of these interactions by the European powers from the sixteenth to the mid-twentieth century, the ancient linkages are, as noted by Duara, being re-established. The "Asia Redux" is the restoration of the connections and connectivities that linked together but went beyond the Asian continent.

Asia Is Not One

AMITAV ACHARYA

Asia is not "one," and there is no singular idea of Asia. Asia is of multiple (although not always mutually exclusive) conceptions, some drawing on material forces, such as economic growth, interdependence, and physical power, and others having ideational foundations, such as civilizational linkages and normative aspirations. Some of these varied conceptions of Asia have shaped in meaningful ways the destinies of its states and peoples. Moreover, they have underpinned different forms of regionalism, which, in turn, has ensured that Asia, despite its fuzziness and incoherence, has remained a durable, if essentially contested, notion.

Before proceeding further, let me briefly comment on the concepts of region, regionalization, and regionalism, the three central pillars of any meaningful discussion of the contemporary idea of Asia. First, our understanding of what makes a *region* has undergone a major change. There is a growing agreement in the literature that (1) regions are not just material constructs but also ideational ones; (2) regions are not a given or fixed, but are socially constructed—they are made and remade through political, economic, social, and cultural interactions; and (3) just like nation states, regions may rise and wither.[1]

---

[1] I have argued elsewhere that regions should be understood in terms of (1) material and ideational—regionalist ideas and regional identity that move the study of regions beyond purely materialist understandings; (2) whole and parts—a regional (as opposed to mainly country-specific) perspective based on a marriage between disciplinary and area studies approaches; (3) past and present—historical understanding of regions, going beyond contemporary policy issues; (4) inside and outside—internal construction of regions, stressing the role of local agency, as opposed to external stimuli or the naming of regions by external powers; and (5) permanence and transience—the fluidity, "porosity" and transience of regions. See Amitav Acharya, *The Making of Southeast Asia: International Relations of a Region*

Prasenjit Duara distinguishes between "region" and "regionalization", taking the former to mean "the relatively unplanned or evolutionary emergence of an area of interaction and interdependence", and the latter as "the more active, often ideologically driven political process of creating a region". While this is a valid distinction, it obscures (although it is subsumed under "regionalization") the concept and practice of regionalism. Indeed, regionalization and regionalism can be separated analytically. The former is normally understood in the political economy literature as market-driven, as opposed to state-led, advance of transnational economic linkages, including trade, investment, and production. Hence, a relevant term here is the "regionalization of production" in East Asia, which was spurred by the southward movement of Japanese companies and capital following the reevaluation of the yen after the Plaza Accord of 1985, which brought South Korea, Taiwan, Hong Kong, Singapore, and other Southeast Asian countries under its ambit and created a de facto East Asian economic region.[2] Regionalism, as it is understood in the political science and international relations literature, implies the deliberate act of forging a common platform, including new intergovernmental organizations and transnational civil society networks, to deal with common challenges, realise common objectives, and articulate and advance a common identity. While much of this can be subsumed under regionalization in the sense that Duara speaks of, regionalization can proceed in the absence, "the more active, often ideologically driven political process of creating a region", especially when the latter entails formal regional institutions. Asia was far into the process of economic interdependence and transnational production networks before the first formal intergovernmental regional economic grouping, APEC (Asia-Pacific Economic Cooperation), was created in 1989. But it is regionalism that brings the notion of Asia alive.

(Singapore: Institute of Southeast Asian Studies and Ithaca: Cornell University Press, 2012).

[2] Mitchell Bernard and John Ravenhill, "Beyond Product Cycles and Flying Geese: Regionalization, Hierarchy, and the Industrialization of East Asia," *World Politics* 47, no. 2 (January 1995): 171–209.

Moreover, in his discussion of the pre-World War II period, Duara sets "imperial regionalism" against the "anti-imperialist regionalization project in Asia." While I agree with this dichotomy, I argue that the anti-imperialist project, which persisted well into the postwar period, was not singular as a source of Asian regionalism. The trajectory of Asian regionalism had varied underpinnings that need to be recognized. While Duara focuses on Rabindranath Tagore, Okakura Tenshin, and Zhang Taiyan, I bring in Aung San, Ho Chi Minh, and José Rizal. The richness and diversity of Asian regionalism cannot be fully captured without looking these Southeast Asian proponents, for it was in Southeast Asia, especially with the establishment of the Association of Southeast Asian Nations in 1967, that regionalism in Asia found its first truly viable expression.

CONTESTED VISIONS

While "Asia" has not lacked protagonists for the past century and half, these protagonists have differed widely in terms of their ideational underpinnings and political goals. Looking at the champions of Asia and their ideas, at least four different conceptions of Asia can be identified in the early post-World War II period. These may be termed *imperialist Asia*, *nationalist Asia*, *universalist Asia*, and *regionalist Asia*. A fifth conception, *exceptionalist Asia*, though already incipient, would emerge later as a major political force.

These categories are not mutually exclusive. Moreover, elements and impulses within these categories may be present to different degrees in a single proponent of Asia. Thus, while Jawaharlal Nehru of India belonged primarily to nationalist Asia, he also identified with universalist Asia (or at least an internationalist) and regionalist Asia. Moreover, these impulses can shift during the course of a political career, and a lifetime.

The first conception, *imperialist Asia* (similar to Duara's "imperial regionalism"), is tied to the hegemonic purpose of great powers, both Western and Asian. While the term "Asia" did not originate with it, Western colonial rule, even though it severely disrupted existing intraregional commercial traffic and helped divide Asia into different spheres of influence, did contribute to the reification of the concept, thereby furthering the cultural and political dichotomy that had developed between Europe and Asia through the centuries, well before the "consciousness of an Asian identity originated [within Asia] largely in reaction to the colonial system and in the common denominator of anti-Western sentiment."[3]

But it was in the hands of an Asian power, Japan, that the imperialist notion of Asia assumed a peculiar prominence, as imperial Japan and its apologists sought to invoke a discourse of pan-Asianism to legitimize its dominance in a way that Western powers in the region had not and other Asian powers such as China and India would not. The dual role of Japan as Asia's saviour and its hegemonic leader was clearly illustrated in the Japanese notion of a Greater East Asia Co-Prosperity Sphere. Encompassing Japan (including the territories of Korea, Taiwan, and Sakhalin), China, Manchukuo, French Indochina, and the Dutch East Indies, this was, of course, not all of Asia, but the "the concept built on pan-Asian notions of an 'Asian community' that had earlier developed in Japan, and which would be extended to Southeast Asian and South Asian if not on the basis of race, then on the basis of a 'common interest.'"[4] Indeed, representatives from all over Asia were invited to the Greater East Asia Conference held in November 1943.

Although it was but one element among Japanese pan-Asianism, it had the most serious impact on the destinies of the Asian states and the lives of their peoples. This was a concept of hegemonic region and regionalism. While it offered a platform for organizing the unity of those incorporated into it, it was not always on a voluntary basis, but coerced. The Japanese imperialist region was marked by a high degree of trade interdependence, and it certainly inspired freedom struggles all over Asia. But in political terms, it degenerated into another form of foreign dominance, no less oppressive than that of the Western colonial powers. Burma's Aung San, who had earlier endorsed the Greater East Asia Co-Prosperity Sphere, and even envisioned "a common defence policy in East Asia as the best guarantee for the maintenance of the Greater East Asia Co-prosperity

[3] John M. Steadman, *The Myth of Asia* (London: Macmillan, 1969), 32–33.

[4] Peter Duus, "The Greater East Asian Co-Prosperity Sphere: Dream and Reality," *Journal of Northeast Asian History* 5, no. 1 (June 2008): 146–47.

Sphere" (Silverstein, 1972: 21), now insisted that "a new Asian order . . . will not and must not be one like the Co-prosperity Sphere of militarist Japan, nor should it be another Asiatic Monroe doctrine, nor imperial preference or currency bloc."[5]

The legacy of imperialist Asia would have a long-term effect, shaping regional perceptions of the superpower rivalry during the Cold War. The Southeast Asian Treaty Organization, although not outright imperial, was perceived as an attempt at neocolonial domination by some sections in Asia, including India's Nehru and Indonesia's Sukarno. It did not last very long, but helped polarise Asia along the Cold War divide, probably disrupting the socialization of China (along with other issues, including the Korean War, the Taiwan issue, and China's own support for communist movements in the region).

Even before Japanese imperialism could sweep through Asia, there emerged another conception of Asia that may be termed *universalist Asia.* Its most eloquent proponent was Rabindranath Tagore, who combined a visceral distaste for nationalism with a passionate belief in the "common bond of spiritualism" among Asia's peoples.[6] Although Tagore did not specifically advocate a political regionalism of states—this might have been premature given that Asia was still firmly under colonial rule—his recognition and intellectual promotion of the spiritual and civilizational affinities among Asia's peoples constituted an alternative conception of Asian regionalism in which societies rather than states take the center stage and that thrives as much as on ideational and cultural flows as on economic links or political purpose.

Tagore was not alone in articulating a conception of Asia that was not premised on a narrow state-centric nationalism; Rebecca Karl has analysed an alternative form of regionalism, much more politically oriented that Tagore's, among Chinese intellectuals "rooted in non-state centered practices and non-national-chauvinist culturalism," that could be

---

[5] Josef Silverstein, *The Political Legacy of Aung San* (Ithaca, N.Y.: Department of Asian Studies, Southeast Asian Program Cornell University, 1972), 101.

[6] Rabindranath Tagore, *Nationalism* (London: Macmillan, 1918).

contrasted with Sun Yat-sen's "state-based, anti-imperialist vision of Asia."[7] This alternative regionalism that Karl speaks of was centred around the ideas and associates of Chinese intellectual Liang Qichao, and the activities of a little-known organization called the Asian Solidarity Society, which was set up in Tokyo in 1907 by Chinese intellectuals, Japanese socialists, and Indian, Vietnamese, and Filipino exiles. An interesting aspect of this regionalism was the recognition accorded to the "first Filipino," José Rizal, as "the quintessential Asian patriot, from which China and other Asian must learn."[8] Although Rizal is better known as a champion of the unity of the Malay race, his message was appropriated by the non-state-centric variety of Asian regionalism.

Tagore's innate universalism put him at odds with the powerful currents of nationalism sweeping Asia, including in the very places the poet visited in his voyages through Asia, and which he imagined as being integral to his conception of Asia. This is not to say that the proponents of a third conception of Asia, which I call *nationalist Asia,* were untouched by universalist values and instincts. Leaders such as Nehru, Aung San, and Sukarno saw little contradiction between nationalism and international cooperation. As Aung San put it, "I recognise both the virtues and limitations of pure nationalism, I love its virtues, I don't allow myself to be blinded by its limitations, though I knew that it is not easy for the great majority of any nation to get over these limitations."[9] Aung San's nationalism, like those of Nehru and Sukarno, could support both nationalism and internationalism, but these figures from Asia's new power elite did not empathize with universalist Asia at the expense of nationalism.

This third vision of Asia, championed by Asia's nationalist leaders such as China's Sun Yat-sen, India's Jawaharlal Nehru, Burma's Aung San, and Vietnam's Ho Chi Minh, was geared toward harnessing Asia's

---

[7] Rebecca Karl, "Creating Asia: China in the World at the Beginning of Twentieth Century," *American Historical Review* 103, no. 4 (October 1998): 1096–97.

[8] Karl, "Creating Asia," 1106.

[9] Aung San, *Burma's Challenge* (South Okklapa, Myanmar: U Aung Gyi, 1974), 193.

rejuvenation to further the retreat of Western colonialism. Before World War II, especially around the time of the 1927 Congress of the Oppressed Nationalities, a number of leaders within the Indian National Congress (a group that was believed to include Mohandas Gandhi, C.R. Das, and later Nehru) supported the idea of an "Asian federation" to organize joint struggle against Western colonialism.[10] Regionalism in this sense was not only compatible with, but also a bulwark for, Asia's restoration and rejuvenation.[11] Certainly Ho Chi Minh was keen to use regional cooperation to further the cause of Vietnamese independence.[12] In a speech to welcome Sarat Chandra Bose, brother of Subhas Chandra Bose at the city hall of Rangoon on 24 July 1946, Aung San stated that Burma would "stand for an Asiatic Federation in a not very, very remote future, we stand for immediate mutual understanding and joint action, wherever and whenever possible, from now for our mutual interests and for the freedom of India, Burma and indeed all Asia."[13]

In September 1945, Ho Chi Minh spoke of his interest in the creation of a "pan-Asiatic community" comprising Vietnam, Cambodia, Laos, Thailand, Malaya, Burma, India, Indonesia, and the Philippines (China, Japan, and Korea were not included in Ho's vision of an Asiatic community).[14] His ostensible goal at this stage was to foster political and economic cooperation among these countries while maintaining good relations with the United States, France, and Great Britain. This was a time when Ho still hoped that the colonial powers, exhausted by war, would voluntarily speed up the process of decolonization. But when this proved to be a false hope, Ho and other Southeast Asian nationalist

---

[10] T.A. Keenleyside, "Nationalist Indian Attitude towards Asia: A Troublesome Legacy," *Pacific Affairs* 55, no. 2 (Summer 1982): 216.

[11] Amitav Acharya, *The Quest for Identity: International Relations of Southeast Asia* (Singapore: Oxford University Press, 2000).

[12] Christopher E. Goscha, *Thailand and the Southeast Asian Networks of the Vietnamese Revolution, 1885–1954* (Surrey: Curzon Press, 1999), 244.

[13] Aung San, *Bogyoke Aung San Maint-Khun-Myar (1945–1947): General Aung San's Speeches* (Rangoon: Sarpay Bait Man Press, 1971), 86.

[14] Goscha, *Thailand and Southeast Asian Networks of the Vietnamese Revolution*, 244.

leaders began considering the use of regional cooperation to oppose the return of European colonialism. This was clearly evident in Ho's letter to the Indonesian prime minister, Sutan Sjahrir, in November 1946 urging cooperation between the two countries to advance their common struggle for freedom. In his letter, Ho asked Indonesia to join him in getting India, Burma, and Malaya to develop initiatives toward a "Federation of Free Peoples of Southern Asia." But Indonesian leaders responded coolly to this idea, apparently worried that cooperating with the Vietnamese communists would give the Dutch an opportunity to use the fear of communism to delay Indonesia's own independence.

Advancing decolonization was a principal theme at the 1947 Asian Relations Conference in New Delhi, the first conference of Asian nations in the post-war period. It was even more central to the Second Asian Relations Conference, also known as the Conference on Indonesia, which was directly and specifically geared toward supporting Indonesian freedom fighters after the second Dutch police action in 1948. Yet, despite all the talk about pan-Asian unity, its proponents were willing to offer only political, rather than material, support for the region's independence movements. For example, India's aid to Indonesian freedom fighters, an exception, was not extended to Ho Chi Minh, much to the disappointment of Ho's supporters.

And these early stirrings of pan-Asianism did not translate into concrete and durable forms of cooperation and institutionalization. There was an uncomfortable sense that the pan-Asianists of India, Japan, and China "were primarily concerned with their own countries," and their "exhortations . . . largely as an extension of their own distinctive cultures."[15] Moreover, Southeast Asians saw in a pan-Asian community, potential for Chinese or Indian domination. As one Burmese put it, "It was terrible to be ruled by a Western power, but it was even more so to be ruled by an Asian power."[16] And the pan-Asian sentiments of India's leaders were stymied by limited contacts with nationalist leaders in other parts of Asia,

[15] Steadman, *The Myth of Asia*, 33.

[16] Henderson, "The Development of Regionalism in Southeast Asia."

misgivings toward the Nationalist government in China, and the rise of anti-Indian sentiments in Burma and other parts of Asia.[17]

While nationalist Asia sought to channel regionalism as an instrument of anticolonialism and national liberation, the fourth vision, *regionalist Asia,* inspired those who wished to use the combined platform of the region's newly independent nation states to seek a collective voice on the world stage. There was considerable overlap between nationalist and regionalist Asia, with Nehru, Aung San, Ho Chi Minh belonging to both. But the regionalists (or the regionalist side of the nationalists) went a step beyond merely securing independence from colonial rule. The logical next step to follow in the pursuit of Asianism was to seek a role in the management of regional and international affairs. As Aung San of Burma put it, "Asia has been rejuvenated and is progressively coming into world politics. Asia can no longer be ignored in international councils. Its voice grows louder and louder. You can hear it in Indonesia, you can hear it in Indo-China, you can harken to it in Burma and India and elsewhere."[18] One major example of this shift was the differences in the agendas of the Asian Relations Conferences of 1947 and 1949, and that of the Asia-Africa Conference in 1955, which, despite its hybrid name, was thoroughly dominated by the Asians. While the Asian Relations Conferences fretted over support for decolonization, the twenty-nine participants at Bandung, as its secretary-general would put it, set out "to determine . . . the standards and procedures of present-day international relations," including "the formulation and establishment of certain norms for the conduct of present-day international relations and the instruments for the practical application of these norms."[19] In other words, while the Asian Relations Conferences were about independence (from colonial rule), Bandung was about intervention (security from great power or superpower intervention).

The regionalists also saw the possibility of restoring the historical linkages among Asian societies disrupted by European colonialism to forge a regional association. Nehru described the first Asian Relations Conference

---

[17] Keenleyside, "Nationalist Indian Attitude towards Asia."

[18] Silverstein, *The Political Legacy of Aung San,* 101.

[19] Roselan Abdulghani, *The Bandung Spirit* (Jakarta: Prapantja, 1964), 72, 103.

in New Delhi as an "expression of the deeper urge of the mind and spirit of Asia which has persisted in spite of the isolationism which grew up during the years of European domination."[20] We have seen Ho Chi Minh's interest in a "pan-Asiatic Community." Immediately after World War II, Nehru would advocate a regional association: "a closer union between India and South-East Asia on the one side, and Afghanistan, Iran, and the Arab world on the West."[21]

But Southeast Asians were unnerved by the prospects for a larger Asian federation or even association. Even professing deep friendship with India, Aung San recognised that "[w]hile India should be one entity and China another, Southeast Asia as a whole should form an entity—then, finally, we should come together in a bigger union with the participation of other parts of Asia as well."[22] Southeast Asia would find subregional unity more practical and palatable. Bear in mind that José Rizal had advocated the unity of the Malay race, although he was appropriated by pan-Asianists. Frustrated by the failure of his efforts to secure material aid from fellow Asian countries for his struggle against the French, Ho Chi Minh would turn to the idea of an Indochinese federation. "Because of the close geography and extricable relationship in military and politics between Vietnam, Laos and Cambodia, the success or failure of revolutionary liberation of one country will have a direct impact on that of the others. Our task is to help the revolutionary movements in Cambodia and Laos."[23]

This Southeast Asian concern was evident at the 1947 Asian Relations Conference, where Abu Hanifa, one of the Indonesian representatives to the 1947 conference, wrote later that the idea of a wholly Southeast Asian grouping was conceived at the conference in response to the belief among

---

[20] Jawaharlal Nehru, "Inaugural Address," in *Asian Relations: Report of the Proceedings and Documentation of the First Asian Relations Conference, New Delhi, March–April 1947* (New Delhi: Asian Relations Organization, 1948), 23.

[21] Keenleyside, "Nationalist Indian Attitude towards Asia," 216–17.

[22] Amry Vandenbosch and Richard Butwell, *The Changing Face of Southeast Asia* (Lexington: University Press of Kentucky, 1966), 341.

[23] Ho Chi Minh, *Ho Chi Minh Talks about History,* trans. Houng Nguyen (Hanoi: Nhà Xuât Bản Đại Học Su Phạm, 1995).

the Southeast Asian delegates that the larger states, India and China, could not be expected to support their nationalist cause. At the meeting, delegates from Indonesia, Burma, Thailand, Vietnam, the Philippines, and Malaya "debated, talked, [and] planned a Southeast Asian Association closely cooperating first in cultural and economic matters. Later, there could be perhaps be a more closely knit political cooperation. Some of us even dreamt of a Greater Southeast Asia, a federation."[24]

And the legacy of Nationalist Asia was too strong and enduring to permit any quick and easy fulfilment of these early efforts at Regionalist Asia, even at the subregional level. These efforts were at best intended to strengthen, not weaken the autonomy of the nation state. ASEAN, as Singapore's Foreign Minister S. Rajaratnam would put it, was intended to serve and strengthen the national interest, not to dilute or compromise it.

ASIA BETWEEN UNIVERSALISM AND EXCEPTIONALISM

After the failure of early Asian regionalism, post-Bandung, the next stage in Asia's nationalist-regionalist construction came in the 1960s. It was a region imagined from one of its subregions, Southeast Asia. Southeast Asia took the helm after the leadership of India and China ended—India's because of internal distractions and rivalry with Pakistan (ironically, a member of the Colombo Powers fraternity), and China's because of its violation of its own pledge of noninterference given at the Bandung Conference (one of the ten principles of the Bandung Declaration). Most important, the Sino-Indian War undermined the claims of both to jointly lead Asia. In the meantime, Japan remained mired in the legacy of its imperial record, hesitant to launch new regional initiatives, especially with a political and security purpose. Moreover, Southeast Asia was itself divided and prone to conflict, both domestic and interstate (*Konfrontasi*). The first attempt to create a regional body, the Association of Southeast Asia (ASA), founded in 1960, failed because it did not include Southeast Asia's biggest player, Indonesia. A second body, Maphilindo (Malaysia, Philippines, and

---

[24] Goscha, *Thailand and Southeast Asian Networks of the Vietnamese Revolution*, 255.

Indonesia), premised on the notion of the unity of the Malay race, and thus recalling José Rizal's identification of the Philippines as a Malay nation, also collapsed over escalating tensions between Indonesia and Malaysia, as Sukarno called into question, with military force, the legitimacy of the Malaysian federation.

Yet even the subregional efforts were held by an underlying conception of Asianness. Thus, despite being an association of Southeast Asia, the ASA's proponents saw themselves as part of a larger Asian cultural, political, and economic context. For Thanat Khoman, the Thai foreign minister and a key architect of the ASA, the association was rooted in "Asian culture and traditions." Describing the ASA as an example of "Asian mutual co-operation," he argued, "For Asian solidarity must be and will be forged by Asian hands and the fact that our three countries: the Federation of Malaya, the Philippines, and Thailand, have joined hands in accomplishing this far-reaching task cannot be a mere coincidence."[25]

After these false starts, one segment of Southeast Asia comprising Thailand, Malaysia, Indonesia, the Philippines, and Singapore finally held together to create Asia's first viable multipurpose regional organization, the Association of Southeast Asian Nations (ASEAN). But even by then, a more powerful force of regionalization, in the sense defined earlier, was emerging in parallel with Southeast Asia's search for unity and identity. This was the idea of a Pacific (later Asia-Pacific) community. Proposed by Japanese and Australian academics and driven by the high economic growth and interdependence among the industrial economies of the Pacific Rim, the idea of a Pacific community finally gave Japan a platform to enter the fray of regionalist Asia, albeit at first through epistemic communities and semiofficial groupings such as the Pacific Basin Economic Council (founded 1967), the Pacific Trade and Development Conference (1968), and the Pacific Economic Cooperation Council (1980).

Initially, this was an Asia-Pacific construct, not Asia. Key roles in developing it belonged to individuals, think tanks, and governments, not

[25] Association of Southeast Asia, Report of the Special Session of Foreign Ministers of ASA (Kuala Lumpur/Cameron Highlands: Federation of Malaya, 1962), 33.

just from Japan but also from outside Asia, especially from Australia and the United States. But the Pacific community idea gradually morphed into the Asia-Pacific (or Asia Pacific) idea, largely because of the need to involve ASEAN members who were deeply suspicious of the project as a move to marginalize the developing nations, and with an eye to China's future incorporation. ASEAN's consent and endorsement was necessary to make it work.

The Asia-Pacific idea would lead in 1989 to the first regionwide intergovernmental institution (outside the Economic and Social Commission for Asia and the Pacific and the Asian Development Bank), Asia-Pacific Economic Cooperation (APEC). Its purpose was not to develop a European Union-like supranational body. But neither was it geared, à la nationalist Asia, to anticolonial or anti-Western objectives. By now, those objectives had receded into the historical background. The new agenda of regionalism was interdependence, not independence. The driver was not anticolonial sentiments, but the quest for growth and dynamism. Although no direct evidence can be provided linking regionalism of the Pacific or Asia-Pacific variety with the region's economic growth (it would be the other way around), there was little question that the idea behind it reflected economic performance and optimism for the future. Moreover, what started as an effort defined mainly in Pacific terms became one in which the Asian element would grow to be the more prominent one.

As regionalist Asia continued to compete with nationalist Asia for the support of Asia's new political elite—undercut, but not permanently extinguished, by the latter—there would emerge a fifth conception of Asia, which might be termed *exceptionalist Asia.* It was the product of the phenomenal economic growth enjoyed by some of Asia's economies. Claims about Asia's distinctiveness had always been around, but they were largely the product of Western Orientalism, which imagined Asia to be exotic, romantic, and subservient. A new form of exceptionalism, constructed by Asia's own power elite, came to the fore in the 1990s, this time based on claims and assertions about how Asian culture underpinned the success of its economies. Exceptionalist Asia proponents were, of course, averse to globalization. They actually thrived on its economic benefits, although they were uncomfortable with the globalization of human rights and democracy.

The term "Asian values" emerged in the 1990s in parallel with the high growth of East Asian economies, such as Japan, South Korea, Hong Kong, Taiwan, and Singapore. This led some commentators, such as Singapore prime minister, Lee Kuan Yew, to associate economic performance with cultural traits and habit. While Lee initially spoke of "Confucian values," this later morphed into Asian values. The list of Asian values varies, but generally includes hard work, thrift (high savings rates), an emphasis on education, consensus, the rejection of extreme individualism, national teamwork, and respect for authority. The term acquired a political connotation when critics viewed some elements of it, such as respect for authority, as a justification for authoritarian rule.[26] Critics argued that what passed as Asian values were in no way special or unique to Asian societies, and that the sheer political and cultural diversity of Asia could permit no such generalization about a set of commonly held values across the region. How can one speak of a coherent set of values that can be uniquely "Asian," and ignore the differences between Confucian, Muslim, and Hindu cultural norms? The Asian financial crisis of 1997 dealt a blow to the Asian values concept, when its proponents, Lee Kuan Yew included, admitted that there could be "bad" Asian values, such as corruption and a lack of transparency and accountability.

Coinciding with exceptionalist Asia, and partly deriving from it, a new form of East Asian regionalism challenged the hitherto Asia-Pacific movement of "open regionalism," setting up a contest of sorts between APEC and Malaysian prime minister, Mahathir Mohammed's East Asian Economic Grouping (renamed the East Asia Economic Caucus).[27] Following the 1997 Asian crisis, the idea of an East Asian community

---

[26] Amartya Sen, "Human Rights and Asian Values: What Kee Kuan Yew and Le Peng Don't Understand about Asia," *The New Republic* 217, nos. 2–3 (1997); and *The Economist,* May 18, 1994, 13–14.

[27] Richard Higgott and Richard Stubbs, "Competing Conceptions of Economic Regionalism: APEC versus EAEC in the Asia Pacific," *Review of International Political Economy* 2, no. 3 (Summer 1995): 516–35.

gained momentum. Its advocates saw East Asia as a "crucial and distinctive region in the world," economically more integrated and politically and culturally more coherent than unwieldy Asia-Pacific forums such as the ASEAN Regional Forum and APEC that include the United States, Canada, and Australia. At 54 per cent of the region's total trade, compared to 35 per cent in 1980, intra-East Asian trade was higher than that in the North American free trade region (46 per cent), and "very much comparable to intra-regional trade in the European Union before the 1992 Maastricht treaty."[28] It is thus East Asia that offers the best hopes for a "bona fide regional community with shared challenges, common aspirations and a parallel destiny" and for the development of a "strong sense of regional identity and . . . consciousness."[29]

So far, East Asian regionalism has turned out to be less exclusivist than initially anticipated, thanks partly to persisting transpacific trade and security dependence with the United States and concern for a rising China dominating such an East Asia—only construct. The inaugural East Asian Summit in 2005 took a functional rather than a geographic view of East Asia by giving a seat at the table to India, Australia, and New Zealand. Now it seems the United States and Russia will be invited as well. But whether the non-East Asians will be assured of equal status within the East Asian community, or will be part of the core group driving the community-building process, remains to be seen. Should the "purist" (Han 2005: 147) view of East Asia prevail, these nations would have good reason to be unhappy over their "second-class" status. And while the broadening of the East Asia Summit might have dispelled fears of Chinese dominance, this could engender Chinese disinterest in the summit process. The key challenge for East Asian visionaries and leaders is to find the balance between Chinese dominance and Chinese disinterest.

---

[28] Haruhiko Kuroda, "Towards a Borderless Asia: A Perspective on Asian Economic Integration," speech at the Emerging Markets Forum, 10 December 2005, http://www.adb.org/Documents/Speeches/2005/ms2005088.asp#_ftn3.

[29] East Asia Vision Group Report, "Towards and East Asian Community: Region of Peace, Prosperity and Progress," 2001, 2, 6, 24, http://www.mofa.go.jp/region/asia-paci/report2001.pdf.

In the meantime, echoes of exceptionalist Asia can be seen in the "Rising Asia" discourse inspired by the massive economic growth, military buildup, and attendant political clout of China and, to a lesser extent, India. While nationalist Asia spoke of Asia's emancipation and reemergence from Western dominance, often in spiritual and moral terms, Rising Asia proponents speak to the possibility of Asia displacing the West from its perch of global leadership. How the Asian powers might cooperate to create a common Asian home, much less an Asian powerhouse, remains unclear in the Rising Asia discourse.[30]

The exceptionalists, out of sheer dependence on economic globalization, are likely to keep their regionalism relatively open. Moreover, civil society in Asia seems more firmly wedded to the universalist values of human rights, democracy, and, increasingly, the environment, which could check the exceptionalists, who would otherwise "Asianise" or truncate these values in support of their regime survival concerns. Hence, the Asia that we see in the coming decades may well be shaped by the contestations and compromises between universalist Asia and exceptionalist Asia. In the meantime, some fear that before the contest is settled, imperialist Asia, with support and sustenance from exceptionalist Asia, especially from within China, might take over and fundamentally reshape the Asian order in the twenty-first century. This will happen if China continues with its relentless rise and imposes a Monroe Doctrine-like sphere over its neighbours. The best hope against this would be the strengthening of regionalist Asia. But as yet, limitations of regionalist Asia abound. Asian regional institutions are still sovereignty bound, unwilling and unable to undertake any major role in conflict resolution. The doctrine of noninterference still remains sacred. It will take time to change these underpinnings of nationalist Asia for a truly regionalist Asia to take over.

To conclude, as a scholar of international relations, I am in general agreement with Duara that a prominent place in the construction of Asia has to be given to regionalism and regionalization. It is heartening to see regionalism and regionalization, which are sometimes thought of as a preserve of political scientists, being viewed as seriously helpful

---

30 Amitav Acharya, "The Idea of Asia," *Asia Policy* 9 (January 2010): 32–39.

tools in analyzing the concept of Asia by scholars from other fields in the social sciences and humanities. Without regionalism, I argue, there might not even be any idea of Asia for us to talk about. Speaking of the idea of Asia, Rebecca Karl shows that "far from always meaning the same thing or even including the same configurations of peoples and states, it has been mobilized for very different purposes at different times."[31] Similarly, regionalism in Asia has not been a singular or coherent set of beliefs. Nor has it been an unchanging phenomenon. It has incorporated and contributed to different conceptions of the region in different times, sustaining Asia's diversity and pointing to alternative futures.

[31] Karl, "Creating Asia," 1118.

Response to Prasenjit Duara, "Asia Redux"

BARBARA WATSON ANDAYA

In his provocative paper, Prasenjit Duara argues that prior to the nineteenth century, the web of maritime trade networks infused the ill-defined area we call "Asia" with a genuine coherence, providing a conduit for cultural flows that readily permitted interactive relationships and the mutual adoption of new beliefs and practices. By the late nineteenth century, however, the imperial powers sought to ensure their global dominance by creating regional blocs consisting of territories that were economically subservient to the metropole. The consequent focus on the establishment of territorial boundaries encouraged a "nationalist congruence between state and culture" that gathered pace over the next hundred years. Only now are we beginning to see an Asia where interdependence and increasing cultural contact, carrying echoes of past connectivities, have opened up new opportunities by which a "transnational consciousness" can and should be encouraged.

While Duara's paper will certainly generate a range of reactions, most scholars would probably agree that a preoccupation with nationalism and the nation state has tended to divide Asia, and that pan-Asianism is one of the many "isms" now fading from our vocabulary. Nonetheless, in the early twentieth century, the notion of a unified Asia did have a powerful hold on elites in Japan, China, India, and Southeast Asia, undoubtedly encouraged by Japan's celebrated victory over Russia in 1904.[1] Accordingly, "Asia Redux" draws our attention to the "cultural movement" of pan-Asianism, exemplified in the writings of Okakura Kakuzo (1862–1913) and in those of his contemporaries, the Chinese intellectual Zhang Taiyan (1869–1936) and his Bengali counterpart Rabindranath Tagore (1861–1941). These three men all thought in terms of a community

---

[1] Rana Mitter and Akira Ireye, preface to *Pan-Asianism and Japan's War, 1931–1945* (New York: Palgrave Macmillan, 2007), ix.

linked by a shared civilization and spiritual values, where the "Asiatic races" formed, as Okakura put it, "a single mighty web." From this perspective, Asian affinities encompassed even religious differences, as Islam could be imagined as "Confucianism on horseback."[2]

In this brief response, I will to turn to Duara's primary argument—that the ways in which "regions" and "regionalism" are conceived tends to follow the dominant modes of "spatial production" in a particular period of time. While Duara acknowledges that attachments to the national state remain powerfully influential, even in this globalizing age, he also suggests that "older Asian models of cultural circulation without state domination of identity" supply a significant "historical resource" through which to explore alternative possibilities of configuring an Asian space.

The idea that the supranational connections of contemporary Asia recall the "interlinked universes" of the past and that understandings of region and regionalism are shaped in a specific historical environment is particularly pertinent in light of current and seemingly universal shifts in religious alignments. As the twenty-first century enters its second decade, it is likely that even the most vehement proponents of secularization theory would accept that we are witnessing a global resurgence of religion.[3] In this context, an examination of religious linkages, whether they are affirming old ties or establishing new ones, provides many different ways of contemplating how "Asia" can be envisaged. On the one hand, religious affiliation, so often an integral element in constructions of cultural identity, has long been implicated in the nationalist project and has repeatedly been invoked to help justify the construction of national boundaries. It is hardly surprising that the "rightness" of religious beliefs endorsed by the nation state has often fostered intolerance for the "other", creating an

---

[2] Okakura Kakuzo, *The Ideals of the East, with Special Reference to the Art of Japan* (repr., Rutland, Vt.: Tuttle, 1970), 3–4.

[3] Peter L. Berger, ed., *The Desecularization of the World: Resurgent Religion and World Politics* (Washington, D.C.: Ethics and Public Policy Center, 1999); and David Martin, *On Secularization: Towards a Revised General Theory* (Burlington, Vt.: Ashgate, 2005).

inward-looking alliance potentially unsympathetic to the tolerance that regionalism requires.

On the other hand, pan-Asianism originated in the idea that a commonality of religious values could strengthen wider connections and, in this sense, rise above the divisiveness of national interests. For both Okakura and Zhang, for instance, Buddhism was eminently suited as a means of conceptualizing a regional coherence because of its deep Asian roots. In contemporary times, the conversations may be different, but expanded channels of information and communication have fostered exchanges that similarly endorse Buddhism as a means of connecting "Asia." Devout Buddhist women, seeking to revive the *bhikkhuni sangha*, thus see the strengthening of links between Sri Lanka and China as a way to further collaboration in joint endeavours.[4] The current focus on "social engagement" in all streams of Buddhism has provided further reason to speak of shared preoccupations in "Buddhist Asia," despite the variety of environments in which Buddhism operates and the ways in which these environments have shaped religious praxis.[5]

Nonetheless, the idea that Buddhism maps easily onto an Asian cultural space is complicated by the rise of new Buddhist movements that have attained global reach, such as Thailand's Dhammakaya, which has branches in more than twenty countries, and the influential lay Buddhist organization Soka Gakkai, which originated in Japan but now has a worldwide membership.[6] Paradoxically, of course, it could be argued that Buddhism's spread has itself contributed to the notion that "Asia" can be defined in religious terms because of the tendency to speak of

---

[4] Wei-Yi Cheng, *Buddhist Nuns in Taiwan and Sri Lanka: A Critique of the Feminist Perspective* (London: Routledge, 2007), 47-51.

[5] Sallie B. King, *Socially Engaged Buddhism* (Honolulu: University of Hawaii Press, 2009), 2.

[6] Ikeda Daisaku, *A New Era of the People: Forging a Global Network of Robust Individuals* (Tokyo: Soka Gakkai, 2006); and Yano Hidetake, "The Propagation of Theravada Buddhism in Foreign Countries: The Case of the Dhammakaya Temple in Thailand," paper presented to the Conference on "Management and Marketing of Globalizing Asian Religions," National Museum of Ethnology, Osaka, 11–14 August 2009.

"Western" Buddhism. Yet the very notion of Buddhism as a framework for conceptualizing Asia remains problematic, as its various paths, most notably the great schools of Mahayana, Theravada, and Vajrayana, are themselves linked to countries and subregions.[7] The boundaries erected by differences in interpretation or area studies help explain the prevalence of terms such as "East Asian," "South Asian," or "Southeast Asian" Buddhism in academic publications.[8] Even a general topic such as women in Buddhism typically has been studied in terms of *nikaya* or in relation to specific national environments.[9] In other words, while Buddhism is seen as the quintessential "Asian" belief system, it has not been able to withstand the reality of difference and the academic propensity to categorize in terms of cultural distinctiveness, ethnicity, nations, or world regions.

Despite Okakura's depiction of "Confucianism on horseback," pan-Asianism is not normally associated with Islam, which developed beyond Asia as it is cartographically represented. However, the concept of "pan-Islam," which attracted such international attention during the late nineteenth century, has a long history, theologically as well as politically. Over the centuries, the possibility of joining a global brotherhood and

---

[7] Richard F. Gombrich, *Theravada Buddhism: A Social History from Ancient Benares to Modern Colombo* (London: Routledge and Kegan Paul, 2006); Anyen Rinpoche, *Momentary Buddhahood: Mindfulness and the Vajrayana Path (Boston:* Wisdom Publications, 2009); and Paul Williams, *Mahayana Buddhism: The Doctrinal Foundations* (London: Routledge, 2008). Cheng, *Buddhist Nuns*, 176-86.

[8] See, e.g., D.C. Ahir, ed., *Buddhism in South-East Asia* (Delhi: Sri Satguru Publications, 2001); Stephen C. Berkwitz, *South Asian Buddhism: A Survey* (London: Routledge, 2010); and Robert E. Buswell, ed., *Currents and Countercurrents: Korean Influences on the East Asian Buddhist Traditions* (Honolulu: University of Hawaii Press, 2005).

[9] Tessa Bartholmeusz, *Women Under the Bō Tree: Buddhist Nuns in Sri Lanka* (Cambridge: Cambridge University Press, 1994); Chatsumarn Kabilsingh, *Thai Women in Buddhism* (Berkeley, Calif.: Parallax Press, 1991); Diana Y. Paul, *Women in Buddhism: Images of the Feminine in Mahāyāna Tradition* (Berkeley and Los Angeles: University of California Press, 1985); and Miranda Shaw, *Passionate Enlightenment: Women in Tantric Buddhism* (Princeton, N.J.: Princeton University Press, 1994).

a worldwide Islamic community has found a receptive audience in Asia, home to most of the world's Muslims. Furthermore, though Islam's universalism has been undermined by the realities of national loyalties, the ideal of a single Muslim society still has considerable traction. Banned in numerous countries, the organization known as Hizb ut-Tahrir thus absolutely rejects the idea of the nation state, for its goal is the establishment of an Islamic caliphate, with one government for all Muslims.

Studies of Islam's global history provide innumerable examples of the ways in which human interactions and the shared memories attached to buildings, graves, and other sacred sites affirmed connections that made up the *ummah*, the great family of believers. Yet visitors to the Indian subcontinent and Southeast Asia repeatedly commented on the localization of religious practices, which could diverge quite markedly from those of the Middle East. At times, some Asian Muslims have accepted the differences between their interpretations of Islam and those of the Islamic heartlands, and have been prepared to tolerate and even defend local practice. Indeed, the idea that Asia might play a larger role on the Islamic stage does have regional moorings. Prior to their World War II occupation of Southeast Asia, the Japanese expended considerable effort to establish their credentials among Indonesian Muslims by emphasising their common Asian heritage, and presenting themselves as the defenders of Indonesian Islam.[10] Less well known is the fact that in earlier years, the Japanese defeat of Russia had fed Malay rumours of Japan's imminent conversion to Islam and its emergence as a new anticolonial leader.[11]

Today, "Muslim Asia" is not a marked category within Asia itself, where there is much greater interest in strengthening links with a global Islamic community. The idea that Islam can help set "Asia" apart is most evident among Western scholars, perhaps eager to separate images of "their" area from what they see as negative portrayals of the Middle East. Despite the vast differences between Taliban supporters in Afghanistan and Cham

---

[10] Harry Benda, *The Crescent and the Rising Sun: Indonesian Islam under the Japanese Occupation, 1942–1945* (The Hague: W. van Hoeve, 1958).

[11] Barbara Watson Andaya, "From Rum to Tokyo: The Search for Anticolonial Allies by the Rulers of Riau, 1899–1914," *Indonesia* 24 (October 1977): 123–56.

Muslims in Vietnam or Uighurs of China, we still find talk of "Asian" Islam as an identifiable category.[12] Even so, undeniable differences in religious observances have made it difficult to do more than offer case studies under a generalized "Muslim Asia" umbrella. Thus, in a manner reminiscent of Buddhism, the idea of "Asian Islam" is difficult to apply except in very broad terms, and academic studies are typically divided into studies of countries or ethnic groups or, at best, the subregions (albeit multifaceted) of "South," "Southeast" Asian, and, less commonly, "Chinese" Islam.[13]

My inclusion of Christianity in this response may well be questioned, as it is not generally regarded as an "Asian" religion, despite the antiquity of communities in eastern India and elsewhere.[14] Today, however, Christians compose the overwhelming majority in the Philippines and Timor Leste, and other countries include large populations—10 per cent (around 24 million) in Indonesia, for example, and about 30 per cent in Korea. In the sixteenth and seventeenth centuries, when Christianity began its slow spread in Asia, it was typically seen in terms of European "ownership"—a local Catholic was considered attached to the Spanish and Portuguese, while a convert to Protestantism had implicitly declared his loyalty to the Dutch. Intensified by colonialism, the idea of European "ownership," with all that this entails, persisted into modern times. Nonetheless, as the twentieth century progressed, long-standing ties to European churches weakened as Asians assumed leadership of their own congregations and many churches became more accepting of inculturation.

Against this background, the insistence on Christianity's cross-cultural and international message has to some degree been qualified by new

[12] John L. Esposito, "Introduction: Islam in Asia in the Twenty-First Century," in *Asian Islam in the 21st Century,* edited by John L. Esposito, John O. Voll and Osman Bakar (Oxford: Oxford University Press, 2008), 3–10.

[13] See, e.g., Dru Gladney, *Muslim Chinese: Ethnic Nationalism in the People's Republic* (Cambridge, Mass.: Council on East Asian Studies, Harvard University, 1996); Gordon P. Means, Political Islam in Southeast Asia (Boulder, Colo.: Lynne Rienner, 2009); David Taylor, ed., *Islam in South Asia: Critical Concepts in Islamic Studies* (London: Routledge, 2010).

[14] John C. England, *The Hidden History of Christianity in Asia: The Churches of the East Before the Year 1500* (Delhi: ISPCK and CCA, 1996).

initiatives from within the region that promote an "Asian" Christianity.[15] It is worth remembering that some of the most successful evangelists in Southeast Asia in the early twentieth century came from India and China, and during the Second World War, Tokyo dispatched Christian Japanese to the Philippines in order to cultivate connections with local leaders.[16] Yet, here again, we see the flexibility of what constitutes "Asia," for the Asian Ecumenical Council has combined the Christian Conference of Asia (which includes representatives of both Australia and New Zealand) and the Federation of Asian Bishops' Conferences (which also incorporates Kazakhstan). However, assertions of an "Asian" Christianity are most forcefully articulated by Pentecostal-charismatic theologians, with their claim to be more sensitive to "third world" spirituality; in 2005, the Pew Forum estimated that about a third of Asia's Christians could be considered Pentecostal-charismatic, and there is even a journal specifically entitled *Asian Pentecostalism.*[17] The similarity of these church environments and the affluent hubs of Seoul and Singapore have enabled new circuits of charismatic preaching that both affirm the regionality of Asian Christianity while simultaneously locating Pentecostalism firmly within a worldwide movement.

Much to the surprise of many observers, religion has not faded away with the expansion of modernity. Duara's paper concentrates on the role of "powerful systems" such as capitalism and international trade in creating the "space" of Asia. From the perspective of a historian interested in cross-cultural flows, I have argued that the academic study of religion has encouraged a tendency to treat "Asia" as a separate domain, despite the theological insistence on universality. Yet the great variation in Asia's religious life combined with scholarly specializations and the boundaries

---

[15] Michael Nai-Chiu Poon, ed., *Pilgrims and Citizens: Christian Social Engagement in East Asia Today* (Singapore: ATF Press, 2007).

[16] Terada Takefumi, "Christianity and the Japanese Occupation," in *Philippines-Japan Relations*, edited by Ikehata Setsuho and Lydia N. Yu Jose (Quezon City: Ateneo de Manila University Press, 2003).

[17] Allen Anderson and Edmund Tang, eds., *Asian and Pentecostal: The Charismatic Face of Christianity in Asia* (Oxford: Regnum Studies in Mission, 2005).

created by area studies means that regional overviews are typically divided into discrete papers on specific groups, countries or subregions. Though studies of regional religious interaction could potentially encourage the "multiple linkages" that Duara espouses, scholarship is still informed by the influence of territorial nation states or the larger blocs endorsed by world diplomacy. Certainly, the long-term effects of the contemporary "global resurgence of religion" within the academy remain to be seen. However, it seems likely that in the twenty-first century, this resurgence will generate continuing debates about what constitutes "Asia" and that participation in these debates will be greatest within Asia itself.

floating. No Gears Shifting

RUDOLF MRÁZEK

It is impressive how, in Prasenjit Duara's paper, Asian regions are understood and presented—in the breadth of the world, not as objects with sharp edges, or compact entities of cultures, economies, and politics, as blocks of which the present and the global so often are still thought to be made. Reading Duara's paper, I was made to think of the successful Japanese architect Fumihiko Maki's recent grand plan for Singapore, the epitome of Asia today, a design conceived not as a space made of buildings, offices, and flats, not of blocks, but of flows—bridges and flyovers, "links," as Maki calls them. These links are there and the most powerful part of the whole, making the city-state space by cutting through it, over the blocks, and along them. The links are empowered to make everything in the city-state face the open, and to move into the open. A skeptic, of course, may ask, "into what open?" Indeed, the "links" of Singapore, at least those already in action, often lead from offices, flats, and blocks into one mega-supermarket and then into another.

The notion of speed came to my mind first as I read the paper—the speed of political movement, of ideology, of development, the myth of speed, the fear of speed, speed continually increasing as well as the possibility of speed deceleration and sudden stops, the history of speed, the structure of speed. In Duara's Asia, I missed most of this. His Asia, the web of it, the model of interconnectedness, "inter-referencing Asia," as he calls it, the intriguing plethora of extraterritorial metropolises, biopolises, fusiopolises, as he presents it (or "Disney Land with the death penalty," as William Gibson might call it), the nebula, in all the intensity and sophistication of Duara's paper, to me, is not much else but floating. No gears shifting.

I can hear too much clicking in this history, the steady rhythm that makes machine owners happy, but that, to me, at one moment becomes uninteresting, at another boring, and yet at another scary. Of course, there is that kind of rhythm, and much of it, in the Asia of today on the move. But the world, also, is bleeding. Wherever I look, and in Asia in particular. How to put this and the clicking together? I would like to know whether it is just me, who, reading papers such as Duara's, eagerly looks for fissures, for wheels that get loose, for history schlepping along "crooked lines," to use Geoffrey Eley's term. Presented with a world that appears like an "amazing apparatus," and Duara's image is close to it, I prick up my ears, to say with Franz Kafka, for a "sound of creaking."

Redux is a term around which one section of the paper and much of Duara's overall argument turns. It may be the problem of rhythm again. After the Enlightenment's up-and-up-and-forward-forever sense of time and history proved a not so truly correct idea, newness came forth as a trick. We have seen in Asia amazing masters of it—Suharto in Indonesia, to take a figure whom I know more about, a dictator who kept himself in power for thirty years through development as this kind of renewal. The theme of *redux* is one of the most serious of modern Asia, and Duara is doing a highly commendable job in being one of the few to touch on it. But again, I miss more "creaking"—perhaps in the vein of John Updike's presentation of the theme, in his uncertain, confused—bleeding, indeed—and quite Kierkegaardian *Rabbit Redux.*

There is no doubt, and Duara says it well, that the world, Asia, and each of its regions down to its tiniest part, is subject to globalization. Yet I would like much more of the mood in the paper of globalization, as Jean-Luc Nancy put it, as "an old animal that is globalising." There are, emerging every moment anew and with speed equal to the speed of globalization, *butt-ends* of the world—"remote corners," as Raden Aju Kartini called them more than a century ago. Globalizing Asia excels in producing the remote corners of the region and the butt-ends of progress, in the rhythm of eternal renewal and, indeed, as redux. If greater concern were given to the matter in Duara's paper, hopefully, it might muddle its logic a little.

Duara's paper is built on consulting many various and different views and concepts of "what is a region," and it also opens a space for their interplay. When the paper approaches the crucial problem of the Asian past and present, and the problem of nation states, however, it becomes assertive. No doubt, there is a good reason behind it, to make the line distinct and clear between what preceded and what now follows, between nation states—also imperialist nation states and postcolonial nation states—and the globalization arena of our age. Yet I suggest that the otherness, contrast between the fortress-like, entrenched, enclosed, and intolerant on the side of the nation states, and the fluidity, openness, interconnectedness on the other side, the side of the present globalism, is overdrawn.

However visible and impressive the nation states' entrenchment qualities have been, as I understand it, they were always nothing but reactions to and reflections of the equally strong (however often much less visible) forces of fluidity and openness. One was born from the other, repeatedly. If this were accepted, analysis might become more fruitful—important qualities of entrenchment might be detected in the flow of globalism—not as mere residue of the nation state past but often as newly born or born again, moving with the movement of globalization, and disturbing its rhythm a little, sometimes out of tardiness, other times as an act of resistance—the butt-ends, the dynamos of history.

Duara's paper shows instructively that overdoing the dichotomy of then and now can make even the fluidity, interdependence, and floating of the present processes in Asia seem hard and mechanical and, for want of a better word, abstract. One should be inspired by the paper to enquire further into how the argument of entrenching *versus* interdependence and flow has existed and worked for a very long time before the term globalization came into use—since, say, 1770, in 1819, 1824, 1870, or 1930. As I write this, I can see the faces of past historians (of Indonesia, for example) who made the dichotomy (or tension, or fissure) an axis around which their concept of history turned—C. van Leur, John Smail, and Oliver Wolters, of course.

A bit in the mood of Kracauer's ragpicker, I find the paper at places a little too elegant. There is one particularly inelegant word these days that to me is loudly missing—*exploitation.* This is not to say that some worrisome matters of the current-Asia human conditions are omitted in the paper. Beginning on page fourteen of the typescript I noted (after about a half of the paper), several grave social problems facing the region listed—environmental degradation, water scarcity, public health—yet not exploitation. How far may this lead us to understanding bleeding Asia beyond the problems' physiognomy? Does not the main question asked in the paper's title give us some opportunity to be, for once, a little less liberal? Too elegantly to my taste, the "grave problems" section of the paper *flows* into a story of a Chinese dam that threatens to divert the waters from where they are needed, and then to the case of Thailand and water problems of this kind. At such a moment, the paper appears to me to be exclusively about the flow and the ways, how not to stand in its way.

With full justification, Duara describes migration as one of the most pressing problems of globalizing Asia today. He touches on the most flagrant aspects of it—elite migrants, immigrant gangs, migrant labour, and domestic workers. Knowledge, business, labour (and crime), again, flow through the time and space, across the borders—the networks are floating. These pages make for absorbing reading. Yet, does not this, again, suggest that the problems of migration are essentially difficulties on the way and, once more, residues of the past, of the fortresses, of entrenchment *still* in place—of outdated nation states (and trade unions, of course, in this logic)? Fear and trembling come over me on the rare but most valuable occasions when, unexpectedly, I am confronted with some new fact about a particular case of a migrant worker, in Singapore, for instance, with some statistics on migrant workers that suddenly appear as if out of context and out of the blue, with each involuntary peep into a maid's living quarters, for example in Jakarta, not to speak about some of the *redux*-new new-Asia sweatshops.

Matters vaguely like those (not the particular cases) come up on page sixteen in my copy of the paper, with a suggestion of a desirable "new relationship between elite and working-class migration." What might in this context the "old relationship" mean? By raising the problem so late into the paper, and by dealing with it in such a fluid manner, I cannot help but feel that the matter of labour, of its structure and rhythm, appears a bit—quite a bit—as an afterthought.

There is a powerful attraction lately to one particular kind of argumentation. The argumentation aims, to put it bluntly, at an "NGO solution," or (if I let myself be carried away) an "ATM improvement." It suggests a globalizing and, at the same time, nonconfrontational way of dealing with it, as pragmatic and, indeed, possible. With this sort of reasoning—and there is a danger in Duara's paper of not resisting it—we can flow, labour can flow like that, too, in a calm and regular stream unless disturbed, made to squeeze into too narrow a riverbed, blocked by nation states, postcolonial nation states, imperialist nation states, residues on the way of globalization. If the residues get excessive, in a disaster scenario, labour may get violent.

With the notion of exploitation missing, in Duara's paper, a progressive tone, a sense of a convincing possible opening, a link-like scenario of the future are allowed to work. Naturally, and Duara duly registers it, globalization also displaces the poor and deepens the gulf between the rich and the non-rich. But globalization, it is made categorical, is inevitable: by its very being, by its producing wealth, by its connecting people. As for that one particular kind of entrenchment—the entrenchment of the elites against the poor—NGOs are expected to take up the job, and to "guard the interests of the regions as a whole." The apparatus will work. The skeleton will be tickled.

* * *

The nineteenth and the twentieth centuries, the paper suggests, were not a time of growing Asian connections. What connections? What about the exploding and imploding of ideas of nationalism, progress, racism, liberalism, and socialism at the time? Not to address these connections, to me, is one of the paper's most unexciting absences.

The connections that are present in the paper and around which the paper's argument is built, are overwhelmingly commercial connections—financial integration, bilateral swap agreements, economic interdependence, coordination so that individual banks do not shoot each other in the foot, trade routes and the interlinked systems of trade routes, mobile merchant communities, traffic that crosses and bypasses economic autarkies, imperial preferences, financial zones and economic blocs. Too much of economics! Yet I am most disappointed when, in the paper, it comes to culture.

Certainly, what Duara highlights in this section has been a significant move of late modern Asian history—the efforts, beginning with the turn of the nineteenth and early twentieth century, to establish an "Asian art," the emergence of Japan as a museum-like sublime and nationalist beacon of Asiatic civilization, alternative Asian cosmopolitanism and pan-Asianism, all this aiming at a congruence between politics and culture, in short, new political homogenization of culture. I understand this, but I have difficulty getting from the paper what might be the internal dynamics (speeding, halting, exploiting) of it, of this new "greater cultural interest of Asians in Asia."

Duara moves into the culture argument of his paper by getting into greater detail. He lists examples, exhibitions, and showings of Asian art, and, as the years and tastes pass by, the circulation of (East) Asian cinema festivals, manga, anime, television shows, Asian eateries—all this is there, and runs through time, speeding and breathing regularly like a well-trained athlete. This is registered. But nothing is there, in the paper, about movements, artists, art consumers, art targets, or art victims such as the contemporary Indonesian painter and dancer Arahmaiani, also a consciousness of the new and globalizing Asia, I am sure, who wanders around the world, anxious about where her home is. She tests the globe for points of shallowness and depth, wealth and poverty, exploitation, possibility of home as well as of interconnectedness.

The phenomenon of Arahmaiani makes me ask troubling questions about Duara's paper. How closely related are "institutions" and "identities"? How derived are they one from the other? How easily can one say of us in this globalizing age, "actual interdependence has increased dramatically and so has cultural contact"? What the dickens may "cultural" mean in this sentence? What may it mean to say that in globalizing Asia, there is "a move away from an essentialist identity formation"?

I believe that it is simply wrong to see the globalization we are currently experiencing as some kind of coming forth of Gayatri Spivak's idea of a liberating and non-Romantic combating "the desire for an origin." Duara argues that consuming Korean television serials by the Vietnamese, for instance, "does not end up transforming an identity from say Vietnamese or Taiwanese to Korean." First, what might "Vietnamese or Taiwanese identity" in this case mean? Second, consumption, voracious or otherwise, of any stuff the Korean television serials has to affect the eater, a man, a woman, and a community. The serials, like the globalism that produces them, to use Marx's expression, "reduce being into having." Or, to quote Heidegger, to the same effect, they reduce the peoples and the world into a "reserve." This, in any case, *is* a new identity.

History, and the hope in it, this is my concluding thought, moves by flowing, linking, and abstracting, but as much as this, also by kicking and resisting the flow, the linking and the abstracting. In some of their best moments, history and the hope in it moves by hesitating about the next step. Presenting modern Asia as being unsure is what I miss most in this brilliant and exquisitely crafted paper.

Response to Comments on "Asia Redux"

PRASENJIT DUARA

Over the last year, as I have presented this paper at various venues, I have received a range of responses. One of them is that this paper is less a disinterested study and more like advocacy. I have hastened to confirm that mine is a position of ethical advocacy, but not without an empirical basis. Objectivity, impartiality, and autonomy from political positions are important ideals in the academic profession, and I count myself among the more enthusiastic supporters of such values. At the same time, I am not so naive as to believe that scholars do not inescapably reflect the intellectual and political positions to be found in the world out there. It is vital to acknowledge this connection because, in doing so, we subject our position and judgement to the scrutiny of their basis in objectivity and accuracy.

What is to be scrutinised are the materials and case I am presenting for a reemergent Asia. My understanding of the material leads me to believe that some form of region making will continue to emerge. Where my personal ethics and preferences play a role lies in my advocacy of one direction among others, that this development could take in the future.

Turning to the question of the ethical aims of such a project, Wang Hui's typically thoughtful considerations give us a good point of entry. Wang appears to be in fundamental agreement with my account, but he seeks to clarify the goals: how can this emergent Asia make a difference? His concluding summary puts it pithily, "the issue of Asia is not simply an Asian issue, but rather a matter of 'world history.'" Reconsidering "Asian history" is at once to reconstruct nineteenth-century European "world history," and an effort to break free of the twenty-first-century "new imperial" order and its associated logic. The critique of Eurocentrism, he argues, cannot be an affirmation of Asiacentrism, but rather an attempt to transform a logic dominated by "egocentrism, exclusivity, and expansionism." I endorse this vision and find it fully compatible with the thrust of my paper.

The regions of Eurasia (or what Tansen Sen calls Afro-Eurasia) have been tied together for more than a thousand years, and "changing gears" in one part of this world has complex consequences in many parts of the rest of it—whether in Asia or Europe. Jack Goody has recently made a persuasive argument that the Eurasian world has been deeply interconnected since the Bronze Age, and no major developments—for instance, the scientific or industrial revolution—can be seen in isolation from these long-term circulations. Rather than focus on radical change or revolution in one part of this world (whether in Western Europe or China), periods of accelerating change in any part of Eurasia have often rapidly affected many other parts. In *The Theft of History*, Goody argues that modern Western scholars have appropriated this common heritage as exclusively Western by a kind of epistemic violence that accompanied and even outlasted Western domination.[1]

In an effort to warn us against further demonization of Western imperialism, Tansen Sen urges us not to neglect violence and domination by historical Asian powers. I would be an utter fool to deny the violence of conquerors, empire builders, plunderers, and pirates. Worse still, any kind of celebratory Asianist essentialism would undo entirely what we have learned from the painstaking work of scholars such as Goody. But denying essentialism does not mean anything goes. I would like to suggest that violence be understood systemically.

By the eighteenth century, global domination and enlightenment came to be packaged in competitive organisms driven, as William McNeill has suggested, by "fiscal militarism" in Europe. Repackaged as capitalist national imperialisms by the nineteenth and twentieth centuries, the institutionalization of competition in the world system wrecked violence, exploitation, and ecological degradation on an unprecedented scale even as powerful forces of creativity and justice were simultaneously unleashed.

Sen also notes that there were landed routes that connected Asia and beyond. I chose to focus on maritime Asia precisely because, following

[1] Jack Goody, *The Theft of History* (New York: Cambridge University Press, 2006).

Janet Abu-Lughod and others, this space seemed relatively free of military violence and control than the landed empires. Sen cites only two major episodes of maritime militarism (Chola and Zheng He) to keep the passages open over the last thousand years. Doubtless there were many more, but this maritime space does not seem to have been as militarized as that of later competitive organisms. The model of Asian connections I am suggesting with its weakly bounded, network-oriented, pluralistic, multitemporal, and issue-based compromises of sovereignty, harks back to this "assemblage" rather than to a competitive and congruent nation state culture. The extent to which this network model can overcome the powerful nationalisms of modern Asian states is still to be seen. But I believe we can see its beginnings, the need and the urge for it.

The papers by Amitav Acharya and Barbara Andaya both contribute to this open-ended and pluralistic conception of Asia. They are entirely correct in pointing to the multiplicity of conceptions—or even regionalizations—of Asia, whether from a political, religious, or some other point of view. Their descriptions enable us to deepen our understanding of Asia as *representation*. In the first place, they represent the multiplicity of responses to a real process of interconnection and interdependence that has no inherent goal. At the same time, they also speak to Gayatri Spivak's comment that "the possibility of the desire for a singular origin is in its iterability" (we want Asia because we can shape it repeatedly).

During the Cold War, Takeuchi Yoshimi articulated this problematic of Asia (as a *desired* signifier of resistance) with his enigmatic call of "Asia as method." More recently, Chen Kuan-hsing has sought to develop this "method" as a form of inter-referentiality where the experiences of neighbours with closely related or intertwined histories may be more suitable points of reference than those from more distant experiences that fill our textbooks and self-knowledge.[2] This superscribed mythic depository of "Asia" may well provide the symbolic underpinning for the emergent regional network. "Asia as method," however, should not be confused

---

[2] Kuan-hsing Chen, *Asia as Method: Toward Deimperialization* (Durham, N.C.: Duke University Press, 2010).

with the more substantive goal of achieving regional sustainability by the critique of rampant capitalism and unyielding nationalism.

Finally, let me briefly respond to Rudolf Mrázek's flamboyant and somewhat oblique critique of my methods. I certainly agree that entrenched institutions, exploitation, and national rivalries persist to a much greater degree than I have attended to here. I have expended much ink over those problems elsewhere. The idea here was to seize hold of an emergent reality and open a discussion about where it may be headed. All in all, I have been more satisfied with this forum than any other in which I have participated. My respondents have engaged with this emergent reality and provoked much critical debate about how we can think about it.

Contributors

JENNIFER MUNGER is the Managing Editor of the *Journal of Asian Studies*.

PRASENJIT DUARA (dprpd@nus.edu.sg) is Raffles Professor of Humanities and Director of Humanities and Social Sciences Research at National University of Singapore. He is also the Director of the Asia Research Institute at National University of Singapore.

WANG HUI (wanghui1010@gmail.com) is Professor in the School of Humanities and Social Sciences, Tsinghua University, Beijing.

TANSEN SEN (tansen.sen@baruch.cuny.edu) is Associate Professor of History at Baruch College, The City University of New York.

AMITAV ACHARYA (aacharya@american.edu) is Professor of International Relations in the School of International Service at the American University.

BARBARA WATSON ANDAYA (bandaya@hawaii.edu) is Professor of Asian Studies at the University of Hawai'i.

RUDOLF MRÁZEK (rdlf@umich.edu) is Professor of History at the University of Michigan–Ann Arbor.

Index

Titles in the Nalanda-Sriwijaya Research Series

Series Editor: Tansen Sen

1. *Preserving Cultural Identity through Education: The Schools of the Chinese Community in Calcutta, India*, by Zhang Xing
2. *Civilizations in Embrace: The Spread of Ideas and the Transformation of Power; India and Southeast Asia in the Classical Age*, by Amitav Acharya
3. *Asia Redux: Conceptualising a Region for Our Times*, by Prasenjit Duara

La vieja del bosque

Ilustraciones: Mabel Piérola

Érase una vez una hermosa joven
que se fue a pasear al bosque
y se perdió.
–¿Qué puedo hacer? –se preguntaba–.
No encontraré una salida
y moriré de hambre.

Al cabo de un rato sintió hambre,
y apareció una blanca paloma
que llevaba una llave de oro en el pico.
–¿Ves aquel árbol? –le dijo–.
Tiene una cerradura.
Ábrela y encontrarás leche y pan
para dar y tomar.
Y así fue.

Más tarde, la joven sintió sueño,
y de nuevo llegó la paloma
con otra llave de oro en el pico.
–Abre aquel árbol y tendrás una buena
cama para dormir –le dijo.
Dicho y hecho.

Al día siguiente, a la hora de vestirse,
la paloma volvió.
–Ahora –le dijo–, abre aquel otro árbol
con esta llave y encontrarás
ropa limpia.

Y así fue pasando el tiempo hasta que,
un día, la paloma le preguntó:
–¿Harías algo por mí?
–Ya lo creo –contestó la joven.

–Te llevaré a una pequeña casa –le dijo–.
Allí encontrarás a una vieja,
con la que no has de cruzar
ni media palabra,
y una mesa llena de joyas.
Busca un anillo y tráemelo.

La joven hizo lo que le pidió la paloma,
pero el anillo no estaba en la mesa.
Entonces, vio como la vieja escondía
una jaula. Se la arrebató
y, en el pico del animal,
la joven encontró lo que buscaba.

Tomó el anillo y salió de prisa
de aquella casa, pensando que la paloma
acudiría en su busca, pero no fue así.
Desolada, se apoyó en el tronco
de un árbol.

Entonces, sintió que el árbol
se volvía suave y flexible;
sus ramas, convertidas en brazos,
la abrazaban dulcemente.
Asustada, se giró y vio a un joven
y apuesto príncipe.

–Una malvada bruja
me había transformado en árbol –le dijo–.
Cada día me convertía en paloma
por unos instantes,
pero mientras ella tuviera el anillo
duraría el hechizo.

De golpe, los árboles del bosque
cobraron forma humana:
eran los sirvientes del príncipe
que también habían sido hechizados.
Cuentan que, desde entonces,
el bosque nunca más fue encantado.

El pequeño abeto

Ilustraciones: Rosa M. Curto

En medio de un inmenso bosque
vivía un abeto muy pequeño
que tenía mucha prisa por crecer.
Sin embargo,
tienen que pasar muchos años
para que un árbol
se haga fuerte y robusto.

Cuando llegó el invierno,
aparecieron en el bosque
unos leñadores
y se llevaron todos los árboles jóvenes
que eran más grandes
que el pequeño abeto.

–Ahora, a tus compañeros,
los venderán por las calles
para que la gente los adorne
y los tenga en casa
durante la Navidad
–le decían los animales del bosque.

–¡Cuánto me gustaría
ser un bonito árbol de Navidad,
lleno de luces y adornos!
–se lamentaba el pequeño abeto
mientras crecía y se hacía fuerte.

Cuando volvió el frío,
aparecieron de nuevo los leñadores
que, esta vez, sí se llevaron
al pequeño abeto.
–¡Qué feliz estará, rodeado de niños
en Nochebuena! –decían los animalitos.

Una vez en la calle
y a la espera de un comprador,
se acercó una niña que exclamó:
—¡Mirad éste! Es precioso,
vamos a llevárnoslo a casa.

Y el pequeño abeto se encontró
adornado con estrellas, bolas
y regalos en el comedor;
justo al lado de la chimenea.
Ahora sí que se sentía importante;
todos lo miraban.

¡Qué feliz era el pequeño abeto
rodeado de niños
que cantaban villancicos!
Le hubiera gustado tanto
que todos sus amigos del bosque
pudieran ver cómo lucía.

Y llegó Nochebuena;
todos cogieron su regalo del árbol
y lo abrieron. Parecían muy contentos,
pero ya nadie se acordaba
del pequeño abeto.

Las hojas del pequeño abeto
se fueron secando y, poco a poco,
se cayeron. Ahora, sin los regalos,
aún se veían más sus secas ramas.
El pequeño abeto se sentía triste y solo.

Pasados unos días,
el pequeño abeto
estaba completamente seco.
Había brillado con todo su esplendor
aquella Nochebuena.
Ahora, convertido en leña,
calentaría la casa
en el crudo invierno.

Blancanieves

Ilustraciones: Javier Andrada

Érase una vez un rey y una reina
que tuvieron una preciosa hija
a la que llamaron Blancanieves.
Poco después del nacimiento,
la reina murió y el rey se volvió a casar.

La nueva reina era una bruja envidiosa
y presumida que a todas horas
se miraba en el espejo y le preguntaba:
–Dime espejito mágico: ¿quién es
la mujer más bella del reino?

–Vos sois la más hermosa –le respondía siempre el espejo. Pero un día le dijo:

–Sois muy hermosa majestad, pero Blancanieves es aún más bella que vos.

La reina, furiosa, tiró el espejo al suelo
y ordenó a un criado de confianza
que llevase a Blancanieves al bosque
y la matara.

Nada más despuntar el alba,
el criado y Blancanieves salieron
hacia el bosque. Pero el sirviente
no tuvo valor para matarla y le pidió
que se escondiera y que nunca más
se acercara al palacio.

Después de vueltas y más vueltas
por el bosque, Blancanieves encontró
una casita donde vivían siete enanitos,
y con ellos se quedó.

Un día, la reina volvió
a preguntarle al espejo:
–Dime espejito mágico:
¿quién es la mujer más bella del reino?
–Sois muy hermosa majestad
pero Blancanieves,
que vive con los siete enanitos,
es aún más bella que vos.

Y la reina, disfrazada de anciana,
se fue a buscar a Blancanieves.
–Toma esta manzana, hermosa niña
–le dijo–. Verás qué dulce es.
Y al primer mordisco,
Blancanieves se desmayó.

Cuando los enanitos
volvieron de trabajar,
creyeron que estaba muerta.
La llevaron hasta un claro del bosque
y la velaron hasta que salió el sol.

Pero de pronto: ¡tararí, tararííí...!;
era un príncipe que iba de cacería.
Cuando vio la hermosura de Blancanieves,
bajó de su caballo, y la besó.

Entonces, Blancanieves despertó
y marchó junto a su príncipe azul.
Los enanitos le dijeron adiós
contentos de verla tan feliz.

Los cisnes salvajes

Ilustraciones: Marina Seoane

Érase una vez un rey viudo
que tenía once hijos
y una hija más bella que el sol.
Pero sucedió que, un día,
el rey se volvió a casar
con una mujer que odiaba a los niños.

–¡Fuera de aquí!
Id a volar por el mundo –dijo
la malvada reina. Y al instante,
los niños se convirtieron
en once bellos cisnes salvajes,
que emprendieron el vuelo.
La princesa se quedó al cuidado
de unos pobres leñadores
hasta que fuera mayor.

Cuando la princesa
cumplió quince años,
la edad de volver a palacio,
la reina le hizo un hechizo
con tres sapos: uno la volvería tonta;
el otro, fea, y el tercero, malvada.

Pero la joven princesa era tan noble
que el hechizo no dio resultado.
Entonces, la reina la despeinó
y la ensució con zumo de nueces
para que su padre no la reconociera.
–¡Echad fuera a esta pordiosera!
–dijo el rey a sus sirvientes
mientras la joven lloraba desconsolada.

La princesa, anda que te anda,
llegó a la orilla del mar.
Estaba anocheciendo cuando,
volando, aparecieron once cisnes que,
una vez en tierra, se transformaron
en once apuestos príncipes.

Entonces, los príncipes explicaron
a su hermana en qué consistía su hechizo:
–Durante el día volamos
convertidos en cisnes salvajes pero,
cuando cae la noche, volvemos a tener
forma humana. Mañana vendrás
con nosotros. Haremos una red con juncos
y en ella te llevaremos.

Y volaron durante todo el día
hasta que pararon a dormir en una cueva.
Allí, la joven soñó
que una bella hada le decía:
–Teje con ortigas once camisas
y extiéndelas sobre tus hermanos.
Así se deshará el hechizo.
Pero mientras tanto, y pase lo que pase,
no debes hablar con nadie.

Nada más despertar,
la joven se puso manos a la obra.
A pesar del terrible picor
que le producían las ortigas,
no dijo ni pío. Ni siquiera abrió la boca
cuando un apuesto príncipe
de gran corazón se enamoró de ella
y la llevó a su palacio.

En palacio, rodeada de comodidades,
la princesa seguía tejiendo y tejiendo
en silencio. Hasta que una noche
se le acabaron las ortigas y tuvo que salir
a por más. Pero por haber salido sola
y de noche en busca de ortigas,
la acusaron de bruja.

—¡Pobre de mí, me quemarán
en la hoguera! —pensaba la joven.
Pese a todo, continuaba tejiendo
sin decir ni mu. Y cuando la condujeron
a la hoguera con sus camisas de ortigas,
once cisnes blancos la acompañaban.

Entonces, la joven lanzó
las camisas sobre los cisnes que,
en el acto, se convirtieron
en once príncipes.
Y todos asistieron a la boda
de su hermana y el príncipe
de gran corazón.